Brick

HENNING MANKELL   THE DOGS OF RIGA

Brick

a literary journal

number 75

summer 2005

PUBLISHER: Michael Redhill

EDITORS: Michael Helm, Michael Ondaatje
Michael Redhill, Esta Spalding, Linda Spalding

MANAGING EDITOR: Rebecca Silver Slayter

ASSISTANT EDITOR: Yohannes Edemariam

DESIGN: Gordon Robertson

COVER & GRAPHICS PRODUCTION: Rick/Simon

COPY EDITOR: Dyanne Rivers

INTERN: stef lenk

VOLUNTEER: Jane Han

WEBSITE: Bitwalla Design

FOUNDERS: Stan Dragland & Jean McKay

Works of art are of an infinite loneliness and with nothing to be so little appreciated as with criticism. Only love can grasp and hold and fairly judge them.

— Rainer Maria Rilke

ISSN 0382-8565, ISBN 0-9687555-9-3
Publications Mail Agreement No. 40042720

Return undeliverable Canadian addresses to circulation department:

BRICK
Box 537, Stn Q
Toronto, Ontario M4T 2M5
Canada

E-mail orders@brickmag.com

We gratefully acknowledge the support of the Canada Council for the Arts and the Ontario Arts Council

BRICK accepts unsolicited manuscripts of non-fiction *only*. Please send submissions with appropriate return postage to

BRICK
Box 537, Stn Q
Toronto, Ontario M4T 2M5
Canada

Submissions may also be e-mailed to submissions@brickmag.com
Subscribe on-line! WWW.BRICKMAG.COM

BRICK is published twice yearly by Cypress Avenue Inc. and is printed and bound in Canada by Transcontinental Printing

Distributed in Canada by CMPA, in the United States by Bernhard DeBoer and Ubiquity Distributors, and in Australia by Pan Macmillan

In This Issue

Cover photo by Dominic Sansoni
Cover designed by Rick/Simon
Brick logos created by David Bolduc

Great writers are either husbands or lovers. Some writers supply the solid virtues of a husband: reliability, intelligibility, generosity, decency. There are other writers in whom one prizes the gifts of a lover, gifts of temperament rather than of moral goodness. Notoriously, women tolerate qualities in a lover . . . that they would never countenance in a husband, in return for excitement, an infusion of intense feeling. In the same way, readers put up with unintelligibility, obsessiveness, painful truths, lies, bad grammar—if, in compensation, the writer allows them to savour rare emotions and dangerous sensations. And, as in life, so in art both are necessary, husbands and lovers. It's a great pity when one is forced to choose between them.

from "Camus' *Notebooks*"
by Susan Sontag

Three Easy Pieces

LAWRENCE WESCHLER

On Coming upon Myself

Each of the presenters at the Chicago Humanities Festival is assigned a host, and mine that year was the exceptionally graceful and gracious art dealer Richard Gray, who, following my little talk, invited me over to his apartment—not surprisingly, an exceptionally graceful and gracious apartment, perched overlooking a gentle bend of Lake Shore Drive, with beyond its arcing traffic, the gleaming expanse of the lake—mainly so that he could show me his collection of old master drawings, which were completely enthralling: old old masters and newer old masters and even a few contemporary pieces, with, coming around one corner, me.

Which is to say, a black-and-brown ink sketch of *mein* very *selbst*, which David Hockney had undertaken a few years earlier when I'd happened to be visiting him at his London digs. Gray beamed triumphantly at my shock of recognition—and indeed, I was completely gobsmacked—but it took me a while (indeed a few days) to work out the exact content of my begobbledment. For it wasn't the only portrait Hockney had ever made of me: over the twenty years that I've been writing about him in magazines and catalogues and books, he has had occasion now and again, here and there, to capture my likeness. Though nowhere near as often as with several of his other regular subjects, whom he has portrayed hundreds of times: a huge swath of his production consists of a record of the gradual aging of that tight-knit community of friends and family—Celia, Gregory, his mother, Mo, Ian, and all the other lovingly rendered likenesses one keeps coming upon at museums and galleries and in books. I'm at best a bit player in their intimate confederacy, and though with the rest of them, I suppose it goes with the territory, it honestly never even occurred to me that any of those drawings of me might ever end up gracing some relative stranger's walls. Who could possibly want such a picture?

Not that it bothered me exactly (it's not that I felt exploited or betrayed or anything like that). I didn't begrudge Hockney the right to spread his drawings about in any manner he saw fit (he'd always made sure to give me a high-quality photo or laser print of any of the pictures he'd made of me). I just felt strange. And it was the precise nature of that strangeness that I kept trying to nail down in the days that followed.

Though I did feel embarrassed, the source of my embarrassment wasn't having my visage up there on the wall, laid bare before the potentially withering evaluations of any of the complete strangers who might have had occasion to pay a call on my gracious host. What did I care what they thought? No, it occurred to me a few days later that what was embarrassing me (and I grant you that this is completely nonsensical magical thinking) was the way that I would be eavesdropping on *them*, that there I'd inevitably be, looking out on the quotidian doings of people whose lives I had no business observing. My host in his skivvies!

I had no idea how such a perverse notion could have entered my head. Except that on second thought, I did. I knew precisely where I'd gotten it from.

Several years earlier I had been doing a profile of Breyten Breytenbach, the great Afrikaner poet and painter who'd served almost eight years as a political prisoner in apartheid jails, during which time his captors had fiendishly forbidden him to paint (fully realizing how, for him, an empty canvas would

have constituted an open field of freedom, a freedom they were intent on denying him). And even though that inability to paint had bedevilled him each and every day of his incarceration, he subsequently found that upon his release, the one place he could hardly bring himself to revisit was his painting studio. For several weeks, he kept circling it skittishly. "I was afraid," he told me as we sat in his studio several months later, "because I hadn't painted for seven and a half years, and with painting, like music, you worry that it's something that if you don't practise it, a lot of it goes—a lot of the technical ability. I was really scared in front of that first canvas."

I asked him if he still had that painting and he said, oh yes; he rummaged around in the back and pulled it out. It was dated February 1, 1983, and the image, quite competently rendered, in dull greys and browns and blues, consisted of a wall, a mirror, and his own face in the mirror, all bruised and pummelled and haggard, with the eyes closed. I asked him why he'd painted himself with his eyes closed, and he replied, "It was all too tender still, I couldn't look at myself yet." (I've often thought about that answer in the years since, and it has seemed ever more astonishing: He couldn't look at himself so he painted a picture of himself with his eyes closed. Who or what in such a situation is looking at whom or what? And who are we, where are we, gazing over the shoulder of that regard?)

Funny, at any rate, the way ideas like that insinuate themselves, transmogrify, and pop up, years later, unbidden: resplendent and bizarre.

Torqued Bruegel

I was going to have to be catching an early afternoon flight out of town, so I'd had to pull a few strings to get in to see Richard Serra's Torqued Ellipses show before the usual 11 A.M. opening time at the Temporary Contemporary, Frank Gehry's converted warehouse exhibition annex of L.A.'s Museum of Contemporary Art.

Perhaps you've seen pictures of those remarkable, monumental pieces. You may even have experienced one or two of them here or there in your own travels. How to describe them, though, to those who haven't? Well, imagine a vast ellipsis—the size, say, of half a basketball court—traced onto the ground. Now, imagine gradually levitating that elliptical shape into the air and slowly rotating it, so that by the time you've got the thing hovering twenty feet above the ground, you've negotiated something like a ninety-degree rotation from its original position. Now, imagine casting the shape across which that form has floated in two-inch-thick corten steel. Slice a narrow vertical passage into the form, so that a person could circumnavigate the whole thing on either the inside or the outside of the wall. And now leave the thing out to rust to a gloriously garish orange-brown. While you're at it, surround its magnificent hulking presence with an even vaster ellipsis, one that you rotate as well, only this time counter-clockwise, providing a narrow vertical passageway on the other side, so that a visitor entering the maze might experience an initially tapered pathway widening as he or she goes along, while the opening above, initially quite wide and expansive, tapers precipitously the deeper in you go,

and then vice versa, until, suddenly, you are delivered into the heart of the labyrinth, that original half-basketball-court-sized elliptical agora, its walls pitching vertiginously from side to side. Way cool.

And now, imagine Serra's having performed a half-dozen variations on that theme and scattering them all about Gehry's vast open hangar space, the lurch and swell and soar and buckle of all that drunken steel.

And then imagine having the place entirely to yourself, as I did for a good half-hour, ambling drop-jawed and woozy from one variation to the next.

A quarter to eleven now, though, and almost time to leave, but just as I was getting set to go, I noticed that a big yellow school bus had just pulled up to the hangar's glass-walled entrance. Its door sprang open and out poured (how to describe *this*?) a teeming Bruegelian throng. A classful of variously misshapen, misbegotten, fate-mangled, brain-damaged, and sight-stunted teenagers, stumbling and gawking and tumbling gleefully into the cavernous hall, one holding onto the next, each having been provided with a musical instrument of some sort—a tambourine or a harmonica or a

Jew's harp or some bongo drums or a cowbell or a whistle—all of them clanging and banging and whooping away, wending their slow, blind progress by means of sound alone: a sheer cacophonous bliss. They'd break off into little strings of marvel, a few heading down one passageway, a few more down another, each experiencing the widenings and tightenings of the surrounding space through the tips of their outstretched fingers and the barometric shifts in the echoing pitches of their instruments alone. The looks on their faces! One boy peeled off, made his way into the heart of one of the mazes, sat himself wedged against the leaning wall and began keening metronomically, forward and then vertical and then *past* vertical—a big broad grin across his face as the back of his skull finally reached the wall with a gently gonging tap: headbanger heaven.

And me, I meandered unnoticed from one group to the next. I remember thinking how I really should get all this down on paper, and then, how no, mere writing couldn't possibly capture it (and I still don't think I have). I wished instead that I'd had a video camera; this would have made a great movie—only, a silent one, so that viewers might have been vouched the exact opposite experience of those enthralled kids.

Mainly, though, I wished that Serra could have been there to see it.

Motes in the Light

One balmy evening late last summer, my friend John and I drove over to the St. Anne's Warehouse performance space, slotted snug under the Brooklyn Bridge overpass on the Brooklyn side of the East River waterfront, to see a screening of Bill Morrison's *Decasia* the way it was meant to be seen. Which is to say with Michael Gordon's astonishing symphonic score being performed live by an orchestra ranged on scaffolds, one row of instrumentalists atop the next, behind three translucent screens, which had been arrayed in a sort of triangle, the audience seated on the floor inside, with three separate versions of the film being projected onto the three screens in slightly staggered fashion—their intersecting cones of light expanding through the smoky air above us—and a conductor energetically directing the proceedings from her precarious perch on a sort of gangplank thrust out above it all. As some of *Brick*'s readers may already know, Morrison has fashioned his film entirely out of snippets of severely distressed and heart-rendingly decomposed nitrate film stock: decades-old footage, wrested, it seems, from archives all around the country—and at the last possible moment. The sort of thing you hear about all the time from crusading preservationists understandably desperate to rescue the world's rapidly self-immolating film heritage—a worthy goal, to be sure—but who knew the stuff was *so beautiful*? That decay itself—artfully marshalled, braided, scored, and sustained—could provoke such transports of sublime reverie amid such pangs of wistful sorrow? And that presented like this, with Gordon's smearily decomposing score lashing the images along, and the players arrayed behind the sweltering screens progressively stripping out of their clothes—the violinists down

to their bras, the hairy-chested tuba player wrapped Laocoön-like in his instrument, the percussionists spraying sweat off their gleaming torsos—the whole thing could pack such a wallop?

A dervish, whirling. A massive bank of film projectors relentlessly unspooling their reels into long canals of developing fluid. A volcanic crater, belching smoke—a craggy shore, the waves breaking (and in turn being broken over as waves of decomposition sweep across the image).

An indecipherable welter of rotted, coursing shapes, and presently, through the pox-veil, a geisha gingerly approaching a screen. A butterfly pinioned against the coruscating surface. A mottled, pullulating mass: the frenzy of moths at twilight. Semen. Cells dividing.

And then later: a procession of camels making their slow way across a desert horizon. Nuns leading their young wards through a mission colonnade. A man rescued from drowning. A grown woman being dunked into a river for baptism. A crouching Central Asian man, spinning wool. A hand-driven Ferris wheel, somewhere in India. And a merry-go-round. A Luna Park rocket car exploding out of disintegrating chaos. A hag pointing a threatening finger at an appalled judge, and then turning back to us, metamorphosing into sheerest monstrosity. Lovers, melting into embraces, which are themselves melting and coming undone. A babe emerging from a womb, and then cradled in a tub of water (developing fluid?). A mine collapse; a shack gone up in flames. A young boxer, gamely jabbing at boiling nothingness. A lonely old man ambling through a mission colonnade.

The empty sky, dappled over with corrosive specks from which gradually emerge sputtering aircraft, droning on, circling, and presently releasing further specks— sperm? No, parachutists, who slowly float down to earth. The projectors unspooling.

The dervish, whirling.

———————

So anyway, afterwards, you can imagine the spent exhilaration with which my friend John and I left the theatre and broached the warm night air, and the sense of baffled slippage with which we now spied another cone of light, this one spreading up from behind and beyond the dilapidated storage buildings between us and the river. We ambled down the block toward the waterfront to get a better view, and suddenly, the entire downtown sweep of Manhattan opened before us, with two beams of light shooting out from its painfully stunted skyline. At which point, we remembered, ah yes, this was September 10, the eve of the anniversary of the disaster.

We joined a small throng gathered there on the waterfront, taking it all in, those two clean beams of light defiantly splitting the night sky. Several individuals were busy taking pictures (several of them, improbably, were using flashes). It took a while for our eyes to adjust, but then things really began to get strange.

Because within the expanding cones of light, tiny scintillating specks seemed to be floating, suspended, like the spangle in an upturned snow globe—flecks, though of what? Confetti? Ashes? Souls? At first the swirl of motes seemed random and limited to the base of the light cones, maybe the first hundred feet above the upturned searchlights. It was hard to tell exactly from all those miles away. But the more we gazed, the more somehow *volitional* their movements came to seem—float, slide, wobble, but then dart and dash. Near collisions narrowly averted; sudden surges straight up. What could they possibly be? Birds? The scale was all wrong, confoundingly so, and there were thousands of them, tens of thousands, and the closer we looked, the higher they seemed to rise, hundreds of yards, all the way up, seemingly miles.

John and I decided to hop into his car, a convertible, to go investigate. We lowered the roof and negotiated the cloverleaf onto the bridge, the same bridge across which all those stunned and shellshocked crowds had trod, in the opposite direction, that skybright morning just short of three years earlier. (Oh, and by the way, can I just interject here that Christo's curtain gates in Central Park this past winter were okay, I suppose, but they had nothing on the thrillingly majestic cavalcade of flexing lines you can experience any day or night of the year on the traverse across the Brooklyn Bridge?) Anyway,

the brilliant motes, carnivalling about in the light beams beyond the bridge cables, seemed no more decipherable the closer we came. Surely they had to be alive, but how could they be soaring like that so high into the sky, and were they huge or tiny or what? Traffic began to bunch up, and it took a good hour on the other side of the bridge to wend our way the last mile toward the bank of searchlights; we had our necks craned the entire while, the solution to the mote puzzle no more apparent. Eventu-

ally, we parked and walked the last few blocks toward Ground Zero. Whereupon, rounding the corner, into that veritable blast of white light, we finally managed to figure it all out.

The motes were *moths*. Hundreds of thousands, millions, of moths, rising thousands of feet into the air. Surely, it seemed, every single moth on the Eastern Seaboard come to pay its respects that gleaming anniversary night.

Sidetracked

CHRISTOPHER ZINN

Steve Earle's cover of "Time Has Come Today" on *Sidetracks* reminds me of the moment in the late sixties when the Chambers Brothers' original version was a hit. Like any good cover, Steve Earle's version makes me hear (and remember) the original in a new way.

I first heard "Time Has Come Today" as a kid, listening to the radio in my room in Pine City, New York. Digression: One of the nicest things my father ever did was to give me a new shortwave radio when I was in seventh grade. And then he strung up a beautiful, hundred-foot antenna from the corner of the house to a big walnut tree in the backyard. I had a weather observation set, too, with an anemometer to measure wind speed. It, too, was connected to a wire, as well as to a blinking light that I could watch in my room. The spinning cups of the anemometer turned a tiny alternating generator, which in turn made the little light blink on and off. The faster it turned, the more rapidly the light cycled on and off. I loved lying in bed counting the beats of the light to measure the wind speed outside, while listening to the radio, also connected to wires outside—and to the ether. I liked to listen to shortwave stations with impenetrable languages, but mostly I listened to AM radio, which, in those great years, was just a revelation. The Beatles one night, the Grass Roots another, and then, the Chambers Brothers. "Time Has Come Today" was convincing, not because of the lyrics, only a few of which I could make out, but because it was sung in this male baritone, black-voiced chorus and had a sound of militancy, and because it referred to psychedelic trippy values, most obviously in the generous use of echo on the vocals. It was spacey and righteous at the same time. It was like hearing Jimi Hendrix for the first time—realizing that black people were *cool* and that they were *turned on*. The song proposed a cultural affinity across the divide of racial unfamiliarity. This was a provincial idea—the idea of a provincial boy—but it didn't mean to be.

Ti–iii–iii–mm-m-e!

Such a cool song, and because it was from the moment of AM, it's also part of widely shared cultural memory, like listening to the Green Berets song. It didn't matter whether you liked it or not. It was there, all around us in the AM airwaves. We lived in a monoculture, but interesting things were crowding in.

Okay, so here is Steve Earle's version, on a collection of his B-sides. It starts out with the same memorable cymbal-and-woodblock ride—the ticking clock rhythm-thought slightly speeded up. And then Abbie Hoffman bursts in unexpectedly—

There's no such thing as a political prisoner— all prisoners are political prisoners, all trials in America are political trials and when you go into jail, you see that, because you see that ninety per cent of the people in jail are black, that's what you see—and you see that ninety per cent of the people are young, that's what you see—and you see that ninety per cent of the people haven't even had a fuckin' trial yet and they're there because they already have so many men in detention, that's what you see in jail. Everybody ought to go there rather than sitting in a fuckin' minimum-security jail like NYU!

And that's just the point, I suppose—this rapid-fire speech about jails is immense because he's haranguing the audience, which you're not supposed to do, but he's also performing, enacting a process of rapid political intellection. He's thinking out loud, in public, about a pressing public issue. And the ideas come so fast; he leaps from one point to the next, but they are all connected by the sense of anger and outrage, emotions that are presented as the key that makes such awareness possible. It's partly about rhetoric and song, since the track meshes the spoken part and the rock part so well. And because he's talking about race and imprisonment, it redirects our understanding of the song to ponder the connection between black political culture and the counterculture. In some sense, it's an accusation that our radicalization was of the "minimum-security" variety, but as the song says, it's also about the ways in which soul was *psychedelicized*. So it's about an old quarrel, but it's also nostalgic for the fire of the sixties, for that sense of urgent cognition and feeling.

And I think Abbie Hoffman is right, after all. It makes me miss him a little.

Writing Kept Hidden

CAROLYN FORCHÉ

The black fire of ink on paper took hold of their souls—incorporeal fire.

And in another part of the city the same happened. One event visible, the other not.

There was no protection this fire couldn't touch nor darkness nor a moment.

It lasted as long as a dream it was no dream. Heteroglossia of nervous shortwave, cloud of blown walls.

In the barracks, those who had sketched themselves in coal and smoke became coal and smoke.

And the living remained, linking unknown things to the known: residue, scapular, matchlight, name on a tongue.

Then, for an hour, the war slept, and rain filled the cisterns with silence.

One who can make himself heard writes: what cannot be said must be written. *Nous sommes de l'autre côté. Nous sommes en face.*

Our windows faced east, and on August evenings, the sky was a blue no longer spoken.

— Beirut, winter 1983

The Dark Art of Poetry

DON PATERSON

It will be blindingly obvious to all of you, I'm sure, that the title of this essay is less a paradox than a nonsense. How can anyone speak openly on a Dark Art? The answer is of course that they can't, or at least shouldn't. And I'm not going to: I have no intention of revealing any of the appalling secrets of my black trade. But I will tell you why I can't, or at least shouldn't.

Perhaps "Occult Science" is a more accurate description than "Dark Art." Poetry is a form of magic, because it tries to change the way we perceive the world; that is to say that it aims to make the texture of our perception malleable. It does so by surreptitious and devious means, by seeding and planting things in the memory and imagination of the reader with such force and insidious originality that they cannot be deprogrammed; what you remember changes how you think. This is where the science comes in. As a science, however, poetry usually fails, because most poets are bad at it. Nonetheless an occult science is exactly what the practice—as distinct from the study—of poetry is.

There are dangers in committing bad things to memory. About a hundred years ago, the mathematician Charles Hinton devised a series of three-dimensional geometrical objects, known as Hinton's Cubes. Once memorized, they could be mentally reassembled into a 3-D net, and then infolded to produce a 4-D model; this, he claimed, would allow you some conception of four-space. Bizarrely, it actually seemed to work. There were two unforeseen consequences, however. Four-space is not a happy thing to carry around in your head when you have to wake up every day in three-space, put your clothes on in the right order, use the toilet accurately, and place your breakfast in the right holes. But worse, Dr. Hinton had devised no means by which, once four-space was memorized, it might be forgotten again. A few folk went irrecoverably insane, and the cubes were quietly withdrawn from public sale.

I've said this so many times it's beginning to sound a bit self-satisfied, but a poem is just a little machine for remembering itself. Whatever other function a rhyme, a metre, an image, a rhetorical trope, a brilliant qualifier, or a stanza break might perform, part of it is simply mnemonic. A poem makes a fetish of its memorability. It does this because the one unique thing about our art is that it can be carried in your head in its original state, intact and perfect. We merely *recall* a string quartet or a film or a painting—actually, at a neurological level, we're remembering only a memory of it; but our memory of the poem *is* the poem. Poets exploit this fact, and attempt to burn their poems into your mind and so mess with your perception. Poetry's most primitive function (and so, we can probably assume, its earliest) is as a system for the simple storage and retrieval of information, and sometimes its concealment: the poets of certain nomadic Saharan tribes are charged with memorizing the location of the water holes, in a way that will not betray them to others. No wonder that poetry, from the earliest so deeply connected to the world and our own survival in it, was quickly credited with magical powers, and soon took the form of the spell, the riddle, the curse, the

blessing, the prayer. Poems are—and remain—invocatory forms. Prose evokes; the well-chosen word describes the thing, perhaps so well it's *as if* the thing were actually present. But there's no "as if" in poetry. Poetry *invokes*; the memorable word seems to conjure its subject from the air.

So that's the occult part, but I also believe that poetry is a science, and that poetic composition can be studied in much the same way as musical composition, though I think the language of verse composition has been lost, or at least disfigured to the point of uselessness. Poets no longer feel confidently expert in their own subject. The language of academic versification studies and "poetics" is really appropriate only for something that describes the result, not the working practice; the noun, not the living verb. This language always makes the error of talking about the messy, insane process of verse-making as if it were a clean operation. Our business is not with rhyme, but with rhyming; not with metaphor, but with metaphorizing, the active transformation of the image; and there is as much difference between the two as there is between checking the time and building a clock.

Such description as exists of the real composing *process* is couched in the language of the beginner's workshop, with its nonsensical talk of show-not-tell, and "good subject matter"—or the language of self-help. Incidentally, the systematic interrogation of the unconscious, which is part of the serious practice of poetry, is the worst form of self-help you could possibly devise. There is a reason why poets enjoy the highest statistical incidence of mental illness among all the professions. Your unconscious is your unconscious for an awfully good reason. If you want to help yourself, *read* a poem, but don't write one. Then again, I think maybe five per cent of folk who write poetry really want to write poetry; the other ninety-five per cent are quite safe, and just want to be a poet. If they knew what the dreams were like, they wouldn't.

Only plumbers can plumb, roofers roof, and drummers drum. Only poets can write poetry. Restoring the science of verse-making might restore our self-certainty in this matter, and naturally resurrect a guild that would soon find it had some secrets worth preserving.

But the main result of such an empowerment would be the rediscovery of our ambition, our risk, and our relevance, through the confidence to insist on the poem as possessing an intrinsic cultural value, of absolutely no use other than for its simple *reading*. Perversely, it has been the insistence on poetry's auxiliary usefulness—for example, in raising issues of cultural identity, as a form of therapy, or generating academic papers—that has encouraged it to think far less of itself, and so eroded its real power to actually inspire readers to think or live differently.

I wholly agree with the postmodern diagnosis made in the sixties that our poetry was becoming domestic, subjective, and trivial. But if anything, that situation is now far worse. Back then, your post-movement poem about moving the settee was at least *really* about a failed relationship. Crippled by the sense of our own cultural irrelevance, we now write poems about moving the settee that are just about moving the settee—or if you're a postmodern, I guess, about "moving the settee."

(A web of ironization hangs over their whole project—their version of Reagan's Strategic Defense Initiative, offering the same kind of illusory protection from the missiles of the barbarians; if we never really *mean* anything, we are safe from their idiotic interpretations—and guaranteed the incontrovertibility of our own. By "postmodern," I'm well aware we all mean something different. In my own case, I'm referring to that peculiar and persistent brand of late-Romantic expressionism, almost always involving the deliberate or inept foregrounding of form or formal strategy over content—almost in a *proud* demonstration of their anti-naturalism, of the fact the two did not evolve together. Homophonic translations of Lithuanian nursery rhymes; poems freakishly juxtaposing archaic and contemporary registers or mutually exclusive jargons; poems consisting of nothing but seven-letter words, or non sequiturs, or typographical errors; poems whose main subject we ultimately identify as the self-consciousness of their own artifice. It is a project wholly blind to one of the first rules of reading, something any literate, non-practising reader would tell you: that there is nothing quite so boring and predictable as a work consisting solely of exceptions.)

The way forward, it seems to me, lies in the redefinition of *risk*. To take a risk in a poem is not to write a big sweary outburst about how dreadful the war in Iraq is, even if you *are* the world's greatest living playwright. This poetry is really nothing but a kind of inverted sentimentalism—that's to say by the time it reaches the page, it's less real anger than a

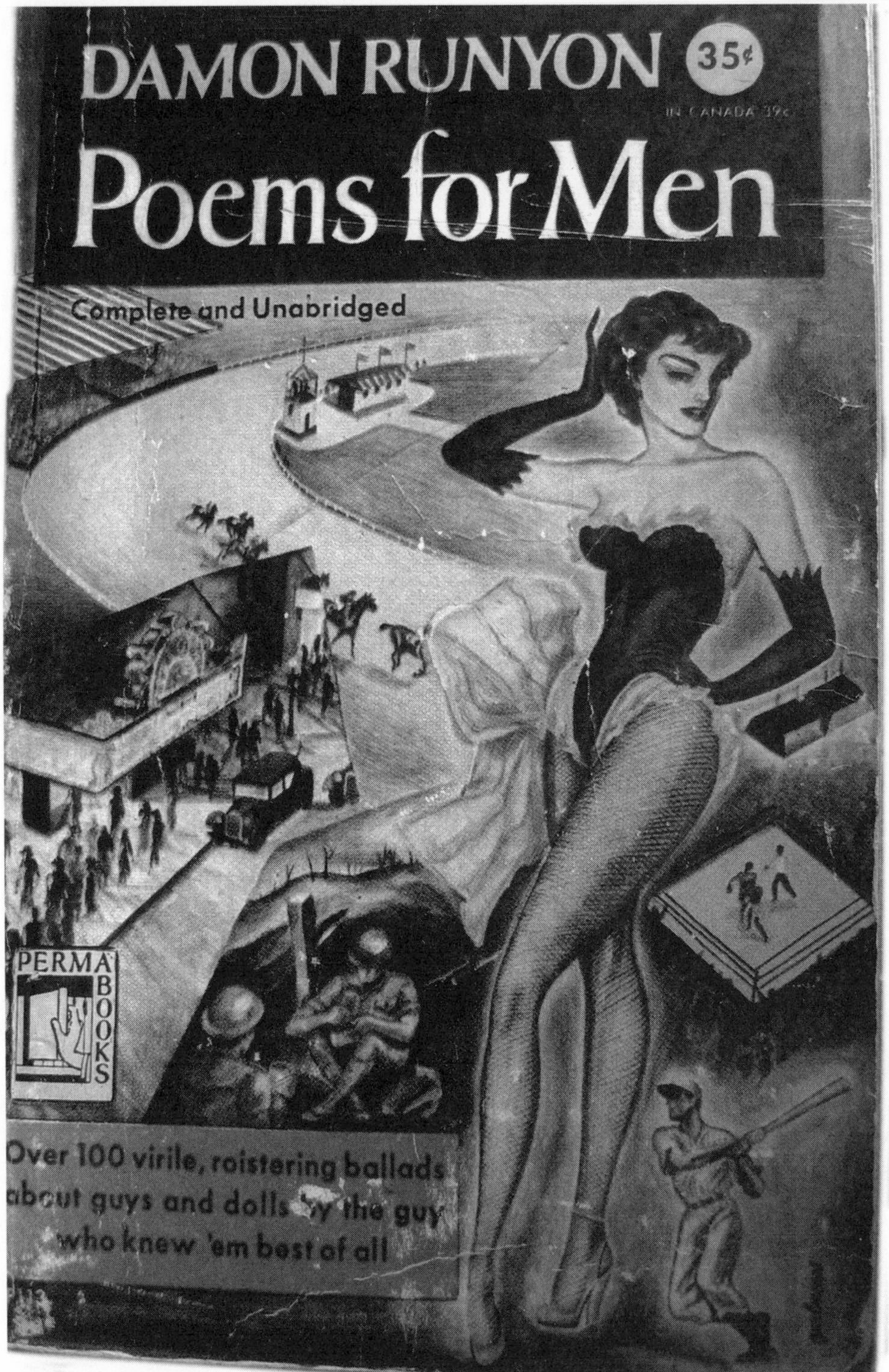

DAMON RUNYON

35¢

IN CANADA 39¢

Poems for Men

Complete and Unabridged

PERMA BOOKS

Over 100 virile, roistering ballads
about guys and dolls by the guy
who knew 'em best of all

celebration of one's own strength of feeling. Since it tries to provoke an emotion of which its target readers are already in high possession, it will change no one's mind about anything; more to the point, *anyone* can do it. Neither is risk the deployment of disjunctive syntax, innovatory punctuation, or wee apropos-of-nothing allusions to Heisenberg and Lacan; because anyone can do that, too. Risk, of the sort that makes readers feel genuinely uncomfortable, excited, open to suggestion, vulnerable to *reprogramming,* complicit in the creative business of their self-transformation, is quite different.

Real danger flirts with the things we most *dread* as poets. Perhaps the biggest risk of all is that of being largely understood and then found to be talking a pile of garbage. But risk is also writing with real feeling, as Frost did, while somehow avoiding sentimentality; with simplicity, as Cavafy did, and somehow avoiding artlessness; daring to be prophetic, as Rilke did, and miraculously avoiding pretentiousness; writing with real originality, as Dickinson did, while somehow avoiding cliché (since, for a reader to be blown away by the original phrase, *it must already be partly familiar to them*, if they are to register the transformation, a point fatally misunderstood by every generation of the avant-garde, which is one reason they are stylistically interchangeable). The narrowest of these paths, though, the poets' beautiful tightrope walk, is the one between sense and mystery—to make one, while revealing the other. As, I think, my friend Michael Donaghy did.

(As someone once remarked, there is no golden mean in poetry. The merely good poem does *not* stand somewhere between the great poem and the bad poem, and is almost another genre. Between the great and the bad, there's a hairline fracture, one we spend our lives trying to map.)

I believe we've become trapped in a vicious circle. The expectation readers invest in us becomes lower and lower by the year, as we disappoint them again and again, whenever they have turned to us, instinctively, for all the old reasons: both to voice and draw out the voice of their fear, love, outrage, and wonder, that their human voice might become woven again into that greater inhuman natural harmony—and, in doing so, find both its sense *and* its mystery.

Our problem is that the roles of poet and reader have become blurred; on the one hand we have the populists, who have made the fatal error of thinking that feeling and practice form a continuum. They infantilize our art: chicken-soup anthologies full of lousy poems; silly workshop exercises where you write a poem in the voice of your socks; ultra-"accessible" poetry programs, where the general public text-message their poems in to be read out on the show. Poetry *is* a wonderfully therapeutic thing to do at an amateur level; but amateur artists and musicians don't think they should exhibit at the Tate or play at the Wigmore. (Serious poets, I should say, don't start off amateurs, but apprentices, just as you would with any other vocation.) The result of the inadvertent democratization of the art has been many people feeling that, armed with a beer mat, a pencil, and a recent mildly traumatic experience, they are entitled to send one hundred pages of handwritten drivel in to Faber or Cape. The myth is that these people are all lunatics. Many of them are well-adjusted, courteous, and intelligent individuals; but writing poetry tends to bring out the worst in almost everyone.

On the other hand we have the postmoderns, who have made the fatal error of thinking that *theory* and practice form a continuum. They don't: this foolish levelling of the playing field in favour of the merely clever has led to an art practice with no effective internal critique. Genuine talents such as, say, Tony Lopez and Denise Riley, working recognizably within the English and European lyric traditions, are drowned by the chorus of highly articulate but fundamentally talentless poet-commentators. Their situation is analogous to British free improvisation in the 1980s, where one could hear great jazz virtuosi like Evan Parker and Derek Bailey sharing a stage with people who had barely mastered the rudiments of their instruments—simply because the valorization of talent *itself* was felt to be elitist and undemocratic. (The thought that some of that art practice afforded the perfect cover for what was, at its worst, pure intellectual charlatanism—well, I'll leave you to explore at your own reflective leisure.)

The populists, on one side, purvey a kind of straight-faced recognition comedy and have no need either for originality or epiphany. On the other side, we have the avant-garde so desperate for transcendence they see it everywhere: they are fatally in the grip of an adolescent sublime, where absolutely anything will blow your mind, as your mind, in its state of recrudescent virginity, is per-

manently desperate to be blown. The Norwich phone book or a set of log tables would serve them as well as their Prynne, in whom they seem able to detect as many shades of mind-blowing confusion as Buddhists do the absolute. Of *course*, we should meet poets at least halfway—the poem, in fact, demands the complicity of the reader in its own creation; however, the amount of running certain readers are making in the relationship should be a matter of mortal embarrassment to them.

Both talk, amusingly, of having struck a blow for the Left, the populists having democratized the art, the postmoderns having subverted the currency of received form and sense, which they see as a kind of capitalist commodification or, in its insistence on finite interpretation, an infringement of their liberties. (Things are much worse in the U.S., where I have been personally denounced as an agent of Rumsfeld and the neo-cons for having suggested poetry might have something to do with interpretable meaning. As someone who thinks of Chomsky as a moderate, I do find this fairly amusing.) But at the end of the day you cannot use the designation *poet* without introducing the highly undemocratic idea of Natural Talent. Poets are people with an unusual gift for the composition of verses. End of definition. Our disagreement, of course, is over what constitutes good verse.

But if you want true "access" to poetry, you have to do two things. First, you have to say who is a poet and who is not. And then you have to simplify the relationship between poet and reader, between whom it should be equal, innocent, responsive and intelligent, where one can educate the other. Wordsworth was not necessarily wrong when he said that every great and original writer must himself create the taste by which he is to be relished, but he should have strengthened that statement. The poet must achieve that alone, with no other apologist or champion but that of his or her own work, through the innocent and direct engagement of simple *publication*.

As an Indian friend said to me the other day— "in this country, you spend a lot of time trying to connect things that are already connected." So here's how you achieve "access": you remove all the mediators. On the one side, those self-appointed popularizers, who, by insisting on nothing but dumb sense, have alienated poetry's natural intelligent and literate constituency by infantilizing our art; and on the other, those exegetes in whose adolescent, retentive self-interest it is to keep poetry as mysterious as possible, that they might project nothing into it but their own wholly novel and ingenious interpretations.

Okay, assuming we've got them out of the way, we close this now smaller gap between poet and reader through publication, a sacred duty and the aim of the poem.

The poem starts as wholly yours and slowly ceases to be so; the process is one of gradual publication, gradual exposure—gradually reading the poem as if it were someone else's, because your aim is to *make* it someone else's.

It starts as inspiration, in the warm, wet, red dark of the brain, and its journey is one of slow separation from its creator, through the stations of,

first, its realization on the page (which is why we so often give them water births, write them in dark corners in pencil or on wee laptops, so they're not shocked by the unfamiliar element. . . . I tend to think of poems as marsupials), through its redaction, its framing or drafting, where you slowly cease to write the poem *you* wanted to and write the one *it* wants to be. At this stage, the poet is switching between a red, wild, creative eye and a blue, cold, editorial one; or amongst the more practised, enjoying a kind of weird blue/red stereoscopic view of the poem—which they are both fully inhabiting and wholly detached from. Toward the end, the poem's consummation, the blue, cold eye is completing the work unaided, according to the poem's by then fully realized interior logic, not the poet's. (All this eye is really saying is "*Would my poem mean the same to me if it were not my poem?*") Then we publish. If the aim is just to finish the poem and not publish it, the poet has configured their relation to it imperfectly from the start. It will never leave their house, never grow up, never speak to another soul, because it never wanted to.

Publication—by which I simply mean "someone else reading your poem"—directly unites the reader and poet, and to read out a line someone else has written in your own voice is to experience a little transmigration of souls. A glorious example of direct publication is Poems on the Underground. The means *is* the end. In a radical subversion of the mechanism of corporate advertising—postmoderns take note—a short good poem is placed in huge type before a person with ten minutes to do nothing else but read it three times, targeting a wide enough audience to find that one in six who is receptive to the high frequency of the art form.

I'd like now to discuss the secret machinery of the relationship between the poem and its reader. This might seem like defining your terms to an insane degree, but when we forget the basics, all discussion of artistic process has a tendency to wander off into self-fascinated irrelevance, particularly in the case of poetry. Poetry is the work of men and women. Men and women are carbon-based, time-based, self-aborting finite projects; they are upright, hairless creatures of the earth, complicated by the highly equivocal gift of consciousness; by this gift, the more awake among them tend to be riven, and at the heart of its paradox must learn to reside—and to think of their consciousness as *other than that* which their instinct often tells them, which is to say a crime against nature. Consciousness has, surely, as Daniel Dennett says, merely evolved. Though our historically unwise decision to stand up on two feet has bequeathed us an increasingly terrible prospect: that of ourselves simultaneously within nature and outside it. Art serves to unite us with what is not us, or rather what we had forgotten was us; it allows us to know ourselves as an expression of the universe, a word of its living speech, not as a book it once wrote and discarded. (In the same way, it is important for poets to see that poetry and its tools—rhyme, lyric, metre, metaphor—naturally arise from the language; they are all natural tendencies in speech; verse merely magnetizes these tendencies to an abstract pattern, to a greater or lesser degree. Poetry is a function of language.)

It's important to remember that our first perception of the world, even one still free from the hysterical labelling machine of language, is *already* a kind of misrepresentation. Incarnated souls all get off to variations on much the same bad start (especially boys, those vessels of karma, whose first act is to *penetrate their mother. . . .*) and are given only the perceptual equivalent of a pinhole camera through which they are supposed to experience the universe. Through this narrow aperture, they perceive a world as only a tiny part of what it is, and even that part, often, as hopelessly subjective and unverifiable. We are born, then, into a condition of metaphor, a metaphor really being a contextual restriction of sense. We are attuned only to a small part of the electromagnetic spectrum, and the universe our senses conjure up for us is not the universe. As Rilke says:

Our senses cannot fathom this night, so
be the meaning of their strange encounter;
at their crossing, be the radiant centre.

Our instruments have long proven this fact—but even on earth we know that the ears of the bat, the eyes of the bee, the nose of the dog, the sensitivity of the bird to magnetic field (to say nothing of the bird's infinite angles of approach to what it beholds, unlike the three ways we have to walk home) shape a perception of the world wholly different from our own, yet no more or less true. We also have the distortions of scale—everything is perceived as either smaller or larger, lighter or heavier, than ourselves—and of time, the perception of the speed of time's unfolding governed by the norm of our own lifespan (and accelerated by our conscious perception of its finitude).

My point here is that even our pre-lapsarian, pre-verbal state is not already without its own huge distortions.

Having fallen into a mammalian dream of the universe, we fall slowly into a much deeper, human dream. The human dream is one of all things first recognized, and then named, in accordance with their human utility, translated and metaphorized

into the human realm. This dream is almost wholly pervasive, so much so that we do not call it a dream at all; we even fall asleep and keep on dreaming inside it. The fact that we corroborate and reinforce the dream-rules in all our human intercourse gives it, of course, the appearance of reality. It is just as flimsy a consensual reality as money. It is a dream.

I'm an admirer of the post-Freudian theorist Ignacio Matte Blanco, and a travesty of his position is this: when we were born, everything was pretty much everything else. The breast was you, your mother the sky, the back garden your mother—the world was an absolute and indivisible unity. There was nothing to tell you otherwise. This perception is atemporal, since the perception of the *passing* and measurement of time, as opposed to the experience of time itself, is dependent first on the perception of difference, of an asymmetrical and consecutive series of events, of which we were not then in possession.

Our perception of things and their relations to one another as wholly symmetrical—less part of a unity than just the unity itself—was gradually overlaid with the perception of linear, discrete, causally successive, and asymmetrical things and events. With the acquisition of language, this goes into overdrive. Now here's the important part: this perception is *not* a refutation of the observations of the first, but a necessary accommodation of the fact of our consciousness. That is to say, the fall into language—asymmetry, the observation that we are *other* than the breast, the mother, and the back garden, the moon, the sea—does *not* occur at the expense of that first knowledge, of everything as everything else, of a unity; this continues running, mostly under the limen of our consciousness, as a kind of spiritual DOS program. Why? Because it was *true*.

This is easy enough to verify. We know what nonsense we can make of a word when we repeat it over and over and strip it of its meaning; that is to say, strip it of *our* meaning. We can do the same with objects. If we remove ourselves from them— if we strip them of the human dream—we can sometimes sneak back quietly to see in the cup, the bath, the shoe, the bicycle, how many strange, lonely, and often ugly things we make for the world. But their *sensible* human utility apart, the category-instability of the thing is soon apparent: a chair suddenly looks like firewood when it gets cold enough. If a chair were in an art exhibit, you would be disinclined to sit on it; if it were persistently referred to as a bed, it would start to look like something to sleep in. To a man with terrible piles, certain chairs look like a reproach, and to an alien with no arse, a chair would be an incomprehensible object.

Such meditations also point up a stark difference between the integrity-status of the man-made and the natural. The former has a habit of looking detached and lonely; the latter part of an integrated expression, having won its form and function through the complex and reciprocal pressures of self and environment, and their mutual rhythmic agitation, in a far, far broader and more integrated economy than our own. (The part we have played as a non-integrated part of that natural economy hardly needs comment.)

I've always felt that every morning the poet should stand at the window and remember that nothing they see, not a bird or stone, has in its possession the name we give it. That seems a reasonably humble starting point. It also might have serious consequences—something very important for a mammal within and without it—for our orientation in addressing the world, our prepositional stance.

Whether you take this seriously or not, all this, for the poet, is much more than a little perceptual game. When we allow silence to reclaim those objects and things of the world, when we allow the words to fall away from them, they reassume their own genius and repossess something of their mystery, their infinite possibility. Then we awaken a little to the realm of the symmetries again, and of no-time, eternity. The poet's specific talent: when the things of the world (in which we should very much include our own feelings, ideas, and relations with one another) that we have contemplated in this wordless and thoughtless silence re-enter the world of asymmetrical concept, of discrete definition, of speech and language, they return as strangers; and then they declare wholly unexpected allegiances, reveal wholly unsuspected valencies. We see the nerve in the bare tree; we hear the applause in the rain. These things are, in other words, *redreamt*; they are *reimagined*; they are *remade.* This, I think, is the deepest meaning of our etymology as *maker.* One more point: the poem, having been translated from the silence, as my friend Charles Simic puts it, has briefly kept the company of everything, of all natural things, and its desire to then declare a kinship with those things—to become a beautiful man-made natural object, with the integrity, symmetry, and rhythm of the natural—should be no surprise.

So the first thing the poet in the act of composition should always observe is silence. Observe, almost in the religious sense: it's a matter of honouring the silence—of which the white page is both a symbol and a means of practical invocation—in which the poem can ultimately reverberate to its deepest reach. (Space sings: this is why the secret guild of guitarists used to place a horse's skull in the corner of the room, as a sympathetic resonator.) We do this by balancing that unity of silence with a reciprocal unity of utterance; the latter actually has the effect of invoking the former. Poetry is the art of saying things once. After all our other skills are in place, our only task is to avoid understatement and overstatement. It sounds an easy matter, but it's a lifetime's study.

(Incidentally, there are no five-fingered exercises in poetry. Do no exercises—they're totally pernicious. Technique can be studied only in the context of real process, of writing the very best poem you can. This is what I mean by the academic lie: the rules of a sonnet teach you nothing about a poet's sonnet, the one we know from the inside, its crystalline internal pressures, the distribution of semantic weight according to the mysterious pattern of its silences.)

It is our riven condition, though—which Rilke refers to as the double realm (that of a living creature with foreknowledge of its own death,

part-ghost)—that makes us creatures that continually connect between the two worlds, that are in fact *driven* to connect; and I believe poetry is the highest form of that negotiation, from the tiny narrow aperture of the Adamite back to the wide-field Edenic. Poetry, then, remystifies, allows the Edenic innocence, the symmetrical and unified view, to be made briefly conscious and re-entered via the most perverse, but perhaps only, tool for the job: language. Poetry is the paradox of language turned against its own declared purpose, that of nailing down the human dream. It uses new metaphors against the dead ones that form our speech. It attempts to conjure up, invoke, those states and those deep connections that have been excluded by the narrowness of the dream, and so cast out of our language. Poets are therefore, paradoxically, experts in the failure of language. Words fail us continually, as we search for them beyond the borders of speech, or drive them to the limit of their meaning and then beyond it. No wonder we tend to stick together.

So what's the nature of this secret language we would need to restore among ourselves? Well, it would consist mainly of arcana. Real arcana is interesting only in prospect. These formulae *must* be very dull, if we are to do our job of alienating the amateur. Arcana are things as small, specific, useful, and horrible as the Horseman's Word. Actually the Word, which gives the apprentice ploughman power over horses and women when it's whispered in their ears, is also the secret formula for all poems. It was unwisely published in F. Marian McNeill's

The Silver Bough, so now it's in the public domain, you might as well know it. In Scots, it's *twa-in-yin*: two in one.

The object of a poem is to place a new unity in the language (an exploded view, if you like, of a new word) that results from the love affair between two hitherto unconnected terms: two words, two ideas, two phrases, two images, a word and an image, a phrase and a new context for it, and so on. *One* thing is sterile and will result perhaps in some pretty description, but nothing the poet did not know before they started. These are the poems that are *made up*. If two things *don't* exist, there will be no discovery in our process, and hence absolutely no surprise for the reader. (I'll give you a more specific formula: the process of the poem is that of a unifying idea being driven through the productive resistance of the form proposed by the marriage of two previously estranged or unrelated things.)

That's how we know we're reading a good poem: an argument or a story has been quietly but insistently proposed in the opening lines. Listen to these of Donaghy's: "Ever been tattooed? It takes a whim of iron"; "Not in the sense that this snapshot, a girl in a garden / is named for its subject, or saves her from aging . . ."; "Hair oil, boiled sweets, chalk dust, squid's ink . . . / Bear with me. I'm trying to conjure my father, aged fourteen / as Caliban . . ."; "Can I come in? I saw you slip away." You know instinctively that there will be a journey, that the poem possesses a dramatic *teleology*, and you are immediately intrigued. The aim should always be clarity of the highest order—forgive my italics, but this is crucially important, and goes to the

heart of our problem with the modernist legacy—*because it is wholly unavoidable that in the process of saying new things we will generate difficult or unusual language.* We actually strive to do so as little as possible. The *additional* introduction of further confusion, complexity, deceit . . . well, that's just inept; and if it's done wilfully, both wholly perverse, and effortlessly easy to achieve.

Now I've been talking for some time in hippie generalities, so I want to turn to a couple of more specific examples of how *real* poetic technique is different from *post hoc* academic description. The examples are pretty random—we could have looked at others from the sub-sciences of lyric, metre, transformation, kinetic syntax, or rhetoric—but I thought you might be interested by these. Of course, I'm responsibly omitting the real techy stuff that would allow you to go home and blow yourselves up.

Puns and plays on words can be tedious in the extreme; all self-conscious effect serves to lift the reader out of the spell of the poem, so they can give the poet a wee round of applause—and then you've lost them. One exception to this is the etymological pun, which, like all our most effective magical techniques, is too quiet for the reader to hear. This is when we use a word fully conscious of its ancestry; we play not on its present or local ambiguity, but on its history. Etymology is a hugely important area of study for us.

Considered alone, as we know, the word sits at a junction between its diachronic history (its etymology and the history of its usage) and its synchronic relations; through these it arrives at the internal properties it now consensually possesses. But poets do not consider words alone. They consider what happens when words meet other words. They are students of the word in silence, and of the relations that silence proposes.

Nearly all words still carry some shade or tone of their deepest etymology. They reveal this not through their current dictionary definition but through those now distant associates that sprang from the same root, and most importantly, something quite inarticulable: the peculiar and specific regard their fellow words now adopt toward them, a unique attitude they have developed over many centuries. I think poets are like great chess players with language; they look less at the next move, or the next ten moves, than at a Gestalt, at a system of relations, and are instinctively sensitive to the whole invisible net of energies, of attraction and repulsion in the poem—and, like the chess player, to *what constitutes a beautiful move within it.*

Your ears are the most important guide, but etymology can also be a great aid in determining that beautiful move. From it, we learn both a word's ancestors and its now distant cousins. From the Indo-European root *kerd*, meaning heart, we derive *cardiac*, also *core*, and *cordial*; *courageous* is Germanic for heartful; *concord*—two hearts as one; *record*—on the tablet of the heart; *accord* and then *accordion*; *quarry*—the heart of the beast being given to the hounds; we get the Latin *cardo*, meaning hinge, the heart of an arrangement, from which we get the cardinal virtues, upon which the whole of human nature was supposed to hinge . . . and so on.

The deeper our understanding of its etymology, the longer and stranger the shadow the word casts, and the more complex the patterns of overlapping shadows become. Its study increases our sensitivity. Again, this technique is an irrelevance to the readers; but they can feel the difference in the vastly improved lock and fit of our words. This terrifically natural sense of word history is one of the principal reasons Heaney is one of our most acclaimed poets. I think poets should always hear the evening in *west*, see the little man in the centre of the *pupil*, the beardless youth in *callow*, or the terrible star in *disaster*.

Now let's look at another example, another little bit of arcana, this time from the art of rhyme. Rhyme, for us, is a verb. This search for natural rhymes is built deeply into the compositional process, so that the rhymes have a sense of their passive or active engagement with the whole poem; they should either emerge naturally from it or guide the poem onward through the partial dictation of its sense. Terminal rhymes, incidentally, should be like eyes across a crowded room, and should be hunted in pairs. Inept poets fix one rhyme too early and refuse to give it up, and the resulting pair usually has the pathos of an old bloke who has chosen a Thai bride from a catalogue. It convinces no one, and looks even lonelier than before.

There's a little technique in poetry we call pararhyme or consonantal rhyme. The noun definition (i.e., the lie, the "rule" of pararhyme) is: it's when you keep the consonantal signature of the word the same, and are free to change all the vowels. So in *cat*, we hear hard *k* and *t*, and can derive *kite, cute, acute, cockatoo, biscuit, Cato* . . . also, from close consonants, words like *caddy, gâteau, god, Agadoo*. Wilfred Owen used pararhyme beautifully in poems like "Strange Meeting." In our own time, it is to Paul Muldoon what feedback was to Jimi Hendrix; that is to say, an infinitely flexible strategy that allows him to articulate his genius. He has also opened it up for other poets to use, though some have failed to appreciate just how quietly and delicately it must be handled.

Now the strange stuff. In order to find pararhymes, unlike other kinds of rhyme, they have to be sought out much earlier than usual; in fact, they can actively prefigure the whole poem. The ear can hear them, but not hunt for them, so the brain must find them out first. Having generated your pararhymes, you can write the poem around them, and use them as strange stations that the argument or the story of the poem must naturally visit. This defines its structure, and thus, rhyming becomes a wholly structural device.

This is identical to the study of the Torah in Jewish mysticism, in kabbalah. Predating the creation of the universe itself (you'll remember the word came first: *fiat lux* predated *lux*), the Torah is printed without vowels, a block of timeless monolithic consonants into which we breathed vowels as it fell, with us, out of Eden and into time. The standard reading of the Pentateuch, however, is not the only way you can envowel it; the kabbalistic researcher could intuit the secret intentions of the divine by seeking out all the other words he could make with different combinations of vowels.

(Almost exactly the same technique was used by the Sufis in early versions of the Qur'an, incidentally, which also appeared without vowels or diacritical marks.) The same line would then be given many different—and far stranger—interpretations. Thus consonantal rhyme was their main tool in the mystical interrogation of the text.

In our art, pararhyming treats the mind as a sacred book. Once this series of secret cognates has been generated—*kabbalah, cable, quibble, cobble, equable, Keble, cue ball, likeable, blackball, a capella, copla*—they must be made sense of, and connected by the memory and imagination, which they simultaneously interrogate. In this way, a hidden and mysterious narrative is revealed. It's a very disturbing way of discovering things you didn't know you knew, and stories you did not think you had it in you to tell; and finding that everything is already connected. Pararhyme, incidentally, like all technique, is rubbish if you foreground it; it merely distracts. This is one reason Muldoon will sometimes separate his rhymes by a hundred lines or a hundred pages; an alternative is simply not to use them in the terminal position, but to bury them in the line. Who needs to know?

I suspect I have already read too freely from our Masonic grimoire, but let me leave you with one thought.

Our defining heresy as poets is that we know that sound and sense are the same thing. Everyone else thinks them merely related. *We need not connect what is already joined*; to unite things again, we so often have to remove our own clumsy connections, our own redundant mediation. The acoustic and semantic properties of the word are not even inter-changeable for us; they are wholly consubstantial. They arose together, and to talk of one is to talk of the other. We allow our ear to think for us.

To embroider a formulation of Hugh Kenner's: like the musical note, the word is an event in time; and like notes, words can be recalled into one an-other's presence and connected in their sense and mystery by the careful repetition and arrangement of their sounds. This repetition therefore intro-duces a real perceptual distortion: it offers a small stay against the *passage* of time. Just as rhyme has the knack of consolidating sense (so much so, in-deed, that it will find sense where previously there was none—can you imagine an unrhymed *Lear*?), unifying the music of the line is, with good poets, an unconscious default. When we sing something, we make a little more sense of it; and when we want to make the deepest possible sense in a lan-guage, we always find ourselves making a song. Now more than ever, we need to keep singing, and singing together.

Three Photographs from Av Isaacs:
Half a Century on the Art Front

Marcel Duchamp (left) plays John Cage at chess. Av Isaacs and Alexina Sattler Matisse look on

Greg Curnoe

Michael Snow, Av Isaacs, Graham Coughtry, and Robert Varvarande

Three Poems

ROO BORSON

Tengluo: **Wisteria**

I ask for the Chinese name of that flower and you tell me, then tell me about the sweet that is made for moon-viewing, wisteria blooms soaked in sugar then rolled in dough, so that I forget all about the name and will have to go to the dictionary to look it up. This is in Spadina Village, a cascade of early purple blooms down the whitewashed building across the street, some kind of a bar or bistro. This is how it goes: inside you there are pictures and in me there are others. Here is the shrub that is translated as plum, though we would never call it a plum except in translation. You ask if there's a word for unspoken understanding, but as usual in English there's no single word, even "silent transmission" is two, though it's often pictured as moonlight, that sudden. In any case, much of the time it is a subtle *mis*understanding that permeates everything: without misunderstanding there would be no literature, no jokes or puns. This is the flower called bleeding heart: its name reflects its structure, but at the same time refers to the death of Christ. And here is a miniature Korean flag, fallen in the street after the festivities for the World Cup, here the eight basic trigrams that combine to form all possible circumstances. You plant it upright in someone's lawn and it stirs to life. Most of us have such great feeling, but the work we do is small. Not much need for talking, but anyway there is talk.

Yuanfen

One day, walking by the Torrens, I met a man. He was coming toward me along the path, and when we were close enough to speak he stopped, setting down in the grass near his feet a small plastic bag he was carrying. He took a moment to clear his throat, and then, in what was clearly his best English, asked whether this was the way to the park.

There are many parks in and around the city of Adelaide, and we were at that moment standing in one of them. He had a street map, he told me (was this the contents of the small bag?), but had chanced upon the river, and now, as it gradually became clear, he wanted to know whether one could reach the city centre by following the course of the river rather than the roads.

One could. He had only to avoid crossing any bridges to the other side, then turn left through the university. . . . We were already nodding our goodbyes when it occurred to me to ask whether he spoke *Zhongwen*, by which, of course, I meant what we call Mandarin.

At once we were on another footing; there was much to discuss. He'd arrived just the day before, and today (being Monday) the friend he was visiting had gone to work, so he'd set out to see the city on his own. That the first person he'd met could speak his own language(!), that both of us had chosen to walk by the river from which neither of us wished to depart. . . . We conducted ourselves word by word, phrase by phrase, making our way back and forth between English and Mandarin largely by guesswork. He appeared to be a little older than I was, possibly in his sixties. This was, I explained, my last day to walk by the river, as the next day we would be leaving for Queensland, then Canada. . . .

No matter! he said, and wrote out his name and address on a scrap of paper. He'd retired to Tasmania for the beautiful view—and indeed, the address he wrote down was a number along View Street. Our meeting, he continued, was *yuanfen*: if you move you must write to me from the new address, if I move I must do the same. People are busy with their own lives, he told me, it doesn't matter if ten or twenty years pass, we can still meet—and next time my English and your Mandarin will both be perfect!

Passing-Cloud Lin, I thought of him for a time, until I was able to consult a better dictionary. Surpassing Clouds, his name seemed to be, Cloud-Transcending Lin.

The feeling of that meeting fades a little each day, though the slight inaudible grinding sensation of the clouds as they pass one another overhead still reminds me of him. And the scrap of paper remains tucked in my wallet, teaching me very slowly, I think, how to live in retirement in the world. *Yuanfen*? I looked it up in the dictionary. It means: predestined affinity, Buddhist fate.

Ba Gua: The Eight Trigrams

I'd been trying to look up a reference to the *ba gua* for my friend Yam Lau, who is interested in such things, but without any luck, for though I'd seen the term mentioned somewhere in the writings of Lu You, and though the partial translation of a diary of his journey down the Yangzi was all I'd read of his work, each time I picked up the book I remained as puzzled as before, and the *ba gua* were nowhere to be found. At the time another friend and I happened to be in the midst of planning our own trip down that same river, to see the famous sights along the banks of the Three Gorges before they too disappeared. One more year and many such sights, including the *ba gua*, would be swallowed up in the damming of the river. But before we could settle on an itinerary, the Yangzi swelled, turning the flood year into one of the most disastrous in decades.

The Yangzi in flood is like a snake swallowing a rat: the bulge moves steadily and swiftly and a very long way before dispersing. The river is so long and its progress so steady that remarkably accurate predictions can be made as to the time of day the floodwaters will reach such-and-such a city three or four days hence. If it's true that what we know of a place veils our eyes before we see it, this must be especially true of those places renowned in literature—and so it may be that, having read Lu You's diary, I've already seen all I will ever know of that region of the Yangzi. In any case, the news clips of the flooding were enough to dissuade us, and so it was that after some time we found ourselves not on one of the great ships that travel the river, but instead crammed into a tiny tourist boat in the middle of West

Lake, veering toward the small islets which in August are willow-green and edged with flowers.

It is a pleasant thing to find oneself in the middle of West Lake in the middle of one's life, to consider the view, and to imagine what is left of one's days stretching out before one toward some imagined horizon, along with the various islets and purpose-built causeways. It must be the effect of this most spacious of lakes in their midst that makes the inhabitants of Hangzhou so serious and easygoing. As one resident, abashed on behalf of his city, and with a beautiful lazy smile, described it, the pace of Hangzhou is "a little slow." In the heat of summer the lakeside paths are crowded with bicyclists and local youth, and with tour groups being shown the sights. The paths are everywhere bordered by flowering gardens, and the gardens are aglitter with butterflies: every flower with its butterfly, and every butterfly a flower, as they say, that has taken to the air. The gardens are adorned with ponds, and the ponds, in turn, with bridges, beneath which the carp gather, opening their mouths in enormous zeroes before the gaping tourists, then winding their way back and forth, braiding the invisible currents with orange blurs and streaks.

Earlier in the day, walking the length of the Bai Causeway, we had stopped for a moment to take a look at the plaque that commemorates the poet Bai Juyi—or was it the Su Causeway, named in honour of Su Dongpo, poet of the Song and governor of Hangzhou, under whose orders this second causeway was built? At any rate, we were hot and thirsty, and a languorous breeze seemed to jostle the words from our mouths as we read. Since coming to Hangzhou, I'd been looking in bookstores for an English version of the works of Su Dongpo, in particular the piece "In Praise of Pork," and so had often thought of Su, a man still revered for his good governance, even a thousand years after his death (something that seems incredible in our age), not to mention his stature as a poet and essayist. Asked about Su that night, and Dongpo rou, the dish named after him, our waiter, in a state of some excitement, hurried off, returning with the manager, who told us, in quite gorgeous English, that it was to Su Dongpo we owed the beauty of the scene before us—cajoling a reluctant populace to take part in the dredging of the lake, their regard for him in this case supplemented by the promise of a dish of Dongpo rou to end each working day. Needless to say, this story proved an excellent enticement, and we ordered Dongpo rou—although the truth, we know, is less fanciful: that local farmers, grateful for the beautification of their lake, made him gifts of pork, which Su, reciprocating, ordered cooked in Dongpo style, inviting everyone to feast.

Hence Dongpo rou, a dish which by its nature would account for Su Dongpo's substantial girth, recorded in the portraits of the time. A small clay pot is placed before each diner; inside each pot a single square of rich pork (the meat interleaved with layers of fat) bubbles in a sauce of dark sweet soy and yellow Shaoxing wine. Even the layers of fat, with the infusion of this sauce, become addictive, so much so that we could well imagine joining the helpless populace reporting to the lake each morning.

Like the carp that follow one another through the water, tourists, as a rule, follow Hangzhou with Suzhou, or vice versa. Even the old proverbs refer to the two, Su-Hang, in a single breath. And so we too moved on, spending several nights in one of Suzhou's tourist inns. Outside our window, green tangerines, another local specialty, were ripening. Suzhou is famous for its canals and gardens: the Garden of the Master of Nets, the Blue Wave Pavilion, the Garden of the Humble Administrator—the latter built in the early sixteenth century by a corrupt Ming official, for his retirement. And indeed, we spent our time there most pleasantly despite the heat, languorously wandering the various gardens, not thinking once of the soon-to-be-flooded Gorges, and the trip we had been unable to take.

Some months after returning from Hangzhou, Suzhou, and the other places we visited, not one of them along the Yangzi, I found myself still troubled, having discovered nothing useful for my friend—beyond, that is, what anyone could find, searching the Internet. That a third-century strategist named Zhuge Liang designed a battle array based on the eight trigrams, the *ba gua*. That this maze-like design had been seen to reappear, century after century, at a particular point along the shoals of the Yangzi whenever the water level was low. That such a marvel could be made to simply vanish from the world—

Still painted on my mind is a picture of the trip we might have taken down that river. I can see us sitting on deck in the river breeze, leisurely peeling the famous oranges that are grown along the banks and tossing the peels to the fish, invisible in those most muddy and jadelike of waters. I suppose there is one Yangzi in Lu You, and that there would be another were we able to look at the river directly, and that these two must perpetually interfere—but it is as though, in my being unable to find it, the reference to the *ba gua* had already disappeared in the floodwaters, either the floods of that year or of the subsequent year, in which the man-made flood would rise and bury all such sights. And then one day, idly dangling my arm over the side of the bed, picking up the book by its cover, I came upon the entry, on the very last page.

I think of my friend Yam Lau in the quiet before snow, adjusting his camera to take a photo of the moon out his window. The moon out his window can now be seen from any computer screen in the world. In some roundabout way, I have him to thank for my trip to Hangzhou. In such a way, at any rate, these thoughts of mine come and go, following one upon another as though intent on some undiscoverable pattern. At times it's as though I'd left myself behind on one of those small garden bridges, or in one of the boats that speed across the mirror surface of West Lake, watching the future all but disappear. But then, to give myself heart, I'll step out for a moment to have a look at what I can only think of now as Yam Lau's moon: worn down to a smooth brilliance, with a tracery of shadows—and the maze, it would seem, is made.

River Writer

KEVIN CONNOLLY

Long considered one of Canada's best poets, Roo Borson was born in Berkeley, California, and emigrated to Canada in her early twenties, living in Vancouver before settling in Toronto. The poems in her first book, Landfall *(1977), made an immediate impact, especially with young writers, among whom (I can tell you from personal experience) it was commonplace to see a poet trying, and failing, to duplicate Borson's spare, direct, and often oddly disquieting lyrics. Six collections, including* The Whole Night Coming Home *(1984) and* Intent, or the Weight of the World *(1989) confirmed Borson as what one critic called "the first major poet to emerge in Canada in the 1980s." But, with the exception of 1996's* Water Memory, *the nineties saw Borson working collaboratively with Andy Patton and Kim Maltman in the poetry collective Pain Not Bread. Last year's* Short Journey Upriver Toward Oishida—*her first new solo collection in almost ten years—won Borson renewed respect, and her first Governor General's Award.*

Borson is probably most commonly thought of as a "nature" poet, but a closer look at her poems reveals an enduring fascination not merely with the natural, but also with our own ambiguous place in it. The new collection (whose title refers to a layover stop mentioned in Matsuo Basho's Narrow Road to the Deep North*) addresses that often awkward relationship more intensely, lit up by the lessons and confusions of mid-life. In it, Borson uses unlineated prose passages that read more like memoir than prose poem, alongside longer, more conversational lyric sequences framed by a series of walks beside rivers in South Australia. In the process, the collection confronts difficult questions about the roles of art, progress, and personal history in shaping a landscape that can't help but reflect us—wounds and all.*

KC: *Short Journey Upriver Toward Oishida* is quite pointedly a mid-life, reckoning kind of book, though I wonder if it seemed like that while you were writing it?

RB: At the time I was very aware of mid-life issues in my life, but I wouldn't say I was aware of writing a mid-life book. I didn't know what kind of book it would turn out to be, and didn't set out with any specific goal in mind. The final result is more a consequence of proximity than deliberation.

KC: The poems that feature rivers are particularly lovely and well written. What struck me repeatedly was how careful you were about making these rivers, and these walks by rivers, so particular, as if you had to work against the supposedly universal. Was that a concern for you, that an image so basic and elemental not wander off into generalities?

RB: Large numbers of the "bits and pieces" were originally composed while walking along the River Torrens (in South Australia), and so the particulars—this willow, that egret—entered naturally. For a long time, I worked on each piece separately, and it wasn't until they began to cohere into a larger structure that I noticed what you could call a thematic presence of rivers, and became alert to the potential problems of either an over-symbolic or over-generic interpretation. Of course, once a willow, an egret, or a river enters a piece of writing, it is no longer that willow, egret, or river. I continued on in the usual way, but keeping my feelers out, trying to stay sensitized. One way of saying this might be that what I wanted, intuitively, was to keep the space inside the book open enough, resonant enough, that it would feel as if those things that were present had been accommodated, rather than incorporated.

KC: On one level, of course, a river unavoidably connotes time, but at the same moment, you insist that the river, and everything in and near it, be nothing but itself. Which in the end makes you wonder if everything, not just rivers, feeds that old argument. Later, you have a very strong line that warrants further explanation: "The past is the past. Yet it is also the present and the future: it is that aspect of the present and the future that cannot be affected by anything we do."

RB: We think of the river connoting time because we've heard the metaphor so often, and the metaphor is at times questionable only because, by now, it's experienced reductively—both elements, time and the river, are taken to stand for little more than an abstract concept of flow. But underneath the surface, the metaphor is still alive. If we can see the river concretely, we can also experience time concretely. If time is no longer seen as a substanceless "flowing past," but as embodied, the freshness returns. Then, whatever exists is *made* of time. But then this way of seeing can get tiresome as well. Maybe literature's "special effects" are generated here, in the dynamic interplay between the abstract and the concrete—sensory experience recombining with conceptual insight to form conceptual experience and sensory insight. At this point in the piece, the narrator is trying to deal with the question of how much one person can or cannot do to help another. Compassion and fear. The young girl who threatened to end her life by jumping into the river has come down from the railing this time, but what of her larger life? What will become of her in the future? Things that have happened to her in the past cannot be erased, and will have effects that are neither knowable nor controllable.

KC: These poems also raise a very resonant question that has to do with the supposed dichotomy between the human and the "natural"—as if there really was one. I think of Pollock's line: "I *am* nature." There's that section in the first poem that has girls throwing bread "across a rusted sign that says Don't Feed the Swans," then the cygnets learning what has bread and what doesn't. In that poem, does it all somehow seem to you to be at least a version of the natural way of things?

RB: I think the perspective that draws a line between the human and the natural has long outlived whatever use it may once have had. But this doesn't mean that whatever humans do—whether viewed as "natural" or not—is automatically excusable. Whether they're aware of it or not, those two girls are negligent in that they're feeding the swans something that will eventually kill them (if they had read the sign they would know this!). This too, as you say, is part of the natural way of things. The girls are doing what gives them pleasure, the cygnets are learning where pleasure lies. The warning exists, inert and unattended.

KC: In the title piece you talk about Basho's tug toward and away from poetry—that feeling that you never want to write another poem again, stalked closely by the other feeling, the promise of accomplishment, that this is what you're meant to do. You say elsewhere that you'd quit poetry twice already. What is it that has made it so difficult for you to write poetry? Was it easier when you were younger?

RB: Writing poetry is exacting and exhilarating at any time of life but, at least in my case, some things have changed. When I was younger, I had the idea that I could make all kinds of mistakes and then "fix" them later in other poems, and to some extent this was true. At midlife, I grasped that the opportunities to fix things were limited, and that whatever mistakes I made now would never be fixed. As a result, I became even more obsessed with revision. At the same time, for a decade I'd been working closely with Kim Maltman and Andy Patton on our collaborative book, and had come to rely on their talents. I'd entered that project at a point when I was tired of my own mind, and now, with the project over, I felt diminished, unsure how to continue, or even whether I had the resources to continue on my own. Add to this a mid-life questioning of the choices one has made, and you can see the situation I was in. But it wasn't just about me. For a while during the nineties, the position of poetry seemed tenuous in Canada, even within the supposed relative safety of the "cultural sector." I remember running into—let's call him X—at York University one day; we had one of those quick conversations, ending with a whispered confidence from X to the effect that poetry was at its *nadir*. Well, it was funny at the time, but also, I feared, true. I think things have picked up since then. Certainly there are plenty of people, including young writers, doing terrific work. Poetry may rise or sink in people's estimation, but it doesn't die.

KC: There's also ambivalence about the function of poetry in this book. It's especially pointed in the piece "A Bit of History," where you discuss the urge the parents of a dead boy have to speak with him in death, to post poems and flowers at the point where he fell from a bridge. You talk about the difference between an artistic poem and a poem written in "commonplaces"—which I think you call a poem that "says what it means." Then you assert that such symbols can be dangerous, "magnets for kids who can see no way out of their difficulties." Can you expand a little on the argument you're having with yourself in that section?

RB: The poems posted on the bridge as a monument to a boy's death, the fact that the young girl considering suicide deliberately made her way to that particular spot, which she obviously knew of in advance—these images pose a question. Certainly the parents of the boy who drowned there have the right to put words to their grief. But then what if the girl had

jumped? Is it possible that the boy's "example" urged her on, confirmed her in the view that suicide is a reasonable way out? But in fact, the narrator only *assumed* that the boy had killed himself, and later discovers the truth, that he slipped accidentally. Does this change the role of the poems on the bridge? And what is the narrator's response? To write a poem! Questions about the function, or functions, of language and of art are good to think about, even if they're ultimately unanswerable.

KC: One of the things that struck me immediately about *Short Journey Upriver* was the counterintuitive treatment of the seasons, and its aptness, at least for someone dealing with grief and absence. "If there were a hell it would be spring, the tortures of the chrysalis, the single suppurating hairs . . ." It's as if spring, with its struggle for breath and life, is too sharp for you, whereas autumn, so dominant here, is a kind of home, or safe house.

RB: For a long time, I felt most at home in autumn, the wild wind and rain. But in the last few years, I've become more and more attached to spring. When I was in my forties, my aunt, who was in her seventies, told me that I was still too young to appreciate kittens! Things seem to even out over a life; there's a strange symmetry to it. But right now, we're probably talking about the four seasons as we know them along the southern edge of Canada. The seasons in one place can be entirely unlike the seasons in another. In South Australia, many native plants flower in the autumn. In the far north of Australia, there are two main seasons: the wet and the dry. I came across a footnote somewhere saying that for a time in China, there were five recognized seasons, the "extra" one falling between summer and autumn, but this may have had more to do with symbolic associations than with the weather. All of China is in a single time zone, but imagine how many kinds of spring and autumn there must be.

KC: If at all possible, can you put into a few words what's wonderful about Australia, what you love about it, and what's disconcerting?

RB: Sulfur-crested cockatoos, galahs, rosellas, lorikeets, kookaburras, casuarinas, banksias, bettongs, pademelons, yellow-footed rock wallabies, spotted quolls, echidnas, goannas, possums, wombats, "sparkies," "firies," "journos," "rellos." All these continue to be odd, though in a lovely way. On the human side, there's a more relaxed attitude overall, a less punishing work ethic, more skepticism and humour. Things that once felt alien about Australia no longer do. I've become acclimatized.

KC: When I read "Persimmons" the first time, I found the sharpness and specificity of the central image slightly distracting, the whole thing almost wanting to be a parable. Then, the second time through, the main current of remembrance and loss took over, and it seemed entirely different, no longer a story, but like someone being in a room with you, telling you something intimate that even she herself doesn't fully understand. How does having lost both your parents now affect your writing?

RB: You are probably in a better position to judge this than I am. Personally, I've never set out to write a piece (or pieces) specifically about my parents' deaths, though events of that magnitude obviously colour everything that comes after them, and it would be strange if this didn't end up being reflected in whatever writing comes afterwards. But the influence for me, in this book at least, is indirect. What you say about your reaction to the piece is interesting, especially if I take it to provide a descriptive category. "Persimmons" has been referred to alternately, by different readers, as a story, an essay, a memoir, and a poem. This pleases me for reasons I wouldn't know how to explain. There's something particularly apt about describing it, formally shall we say, as something which is "no longer a story."

KC: You talk elsewhere about choosing poetry "because it's secret." I'm wondering if there isn't an element of poetry that stays secret from the writer, that a good poem is often a result more of what remains stubbornly unknown.

RB: I agree completely.

KC: Talk to me a little about how this book was written. It gives you the feeling of being composed *en plein air*, on one of your walks, but of course, that's not how it usually works, is it?

RB: You're right. Innumerable walks were involved. And uncountable numbers of revisions, both indoors and outdoors, on paper, on a word processor, and in the air, talking things over with Kim. Walking along the river, trying out phrases every which way. "Summer Grass" was a first sustained attempt at "rehabilitating" myself to solo poetry. Notes for "Persimmons," which had lain in shifting disarray for years, suddenly assembled themselves one day into a roughly coherent shape. The final piece in the book, which revolves around Basho, came out of discussions with Kim on how this book might end; the piece is in many ways a collaborative one. The title was hammered out in a similar way, poring over a map of Basho's journey, and aided by fevered e-mail exchanges with Andy and Janice Gurney, neither of whom had read the book. Andy was concerned that it was a very literary-sounding title, which made me consider its aptness for a book that makes reference to other pieces of writing. Each section took shape in its own way, but then had to accommodate itself to the presence of others. I'd been interested in exploring ways of combining (lineated) poetry with (unlineated) prose, and it seemed possible to make a structure in which pieces with different ratios of these, and using different internal strategies, could come together to make a whole. This kind of language might make it sound like a technical exercise, but there comes a point in poetry when there's no distinction between the personal and the technical. And all along, there were conversations with others, some about issues in the book, but many more about unrelated things, which fed the book in subterranean ways.

KC: Someone once said that you can't really understand a distance until you've walked it. At times while you're walking, you have what seems almost that Buddhist sense of "mindfulness," but then you'll be drawn into the past, and in these poems, usually what's been lost. I wonder if you pondered this relationship between walking and thinking, between repetition and seeing things as they are?

RB: I've always walked a lot. There's a big difference between looking at a photo of a place and being there. The texture and fragrance of the air, the movement of everything. Words rise up, too, the rhythm of walking is a rhythm of poetry. When you walk the same routes regularly, you notice that not only the years but also the days can be subdivided into as many seasons as you like. Nothing stays the same, but there are variations upon variations on a theme that is never stated explicitly, except by us.

How Scientists Party

ALASTAIR BLAND

Every year around finals time, scientists from San Francisco State University gather at the house I was raised in for the Holiday Physics and Astronomy Party. My father, Dr. Roger Bland, a veteran physicist at the university, has hosted this event for the past fifteen years, and I've attended nearly every time. The party, which has achieved near-legend status among the faculty, is a rare opportunity for brilliant scientists and their burnt-out students to mingle, to revel in the underlying silliness of their field, to loosen their neckties after the long semester, to have a few drinks, and to light up the night with electricity and fire.

The first group of guests this year arrived at 7 P.M., tromping in the front door with a spark-generating Tesla coil, a pot of liquid nitrogen, some blowtorches, and a case of Heineken. By 8:30 the alcohol was flowing, the music was thumping, and the whole place was swarming with nerds. There was hardly room to move, yet the throngs parted gracefully for my dad as he made his way from the kitchen to the living room to announce the first event.

He clinked his wineglass with a fork and hollered, "Now begins the Equation-Editing Shootout!"

There were a few cheers, but many of the students looked puzzled. They'd heard about this annual gathering from the old-timers, about how their professors historically got drunk, set things on fire, and acted like delinquents, and they wondered if the party, like an aging rock band, had finally lost its edge.

It was certainly a slow beginning to the famous fete. A Microsoft Word window was projected onto the living room wall as the first contestant, a professor, took a seat at the computer desk. A man with a stopwatch said, "Go!" and the professor began to type. Her goal was to transcribe from a textbook a long and tedious quantum mechanical wave function—and to do it in the least time possible. As a configuration of numbers and Greek lettering began to unfold on the wall, the grad students paid close attention. They sipped their beers and nodded in approval as the equation filled out. It took a full six minutes for the professor to finish, and when she did, there was a round of applause, and a voice shouted, "Yeah! That's what I'm talkin' about!"

I looked up at the screen, but all I saw was this:

$$\Psi_{nlm}(r,\theta,\phi) = \left(\frac{2\mu Z}{m_r a_0}\right)^{3/2} e^{-\frac{r}{a_0}} \sum_{m=0}^{n-l-1} \sqrt{\frac{2n+1}{4\pi}\frac{(n-m)!}{(n+m)!}} \left(1-x^2\right)^{m/2} e^{im\phi}$$

In past years at the Physics and Astronomy Party, I've seen Ph.D.s get high on helium, vacuum-sealed oil drums collapse under the weight of our atmosphere, a giant weather balloon expand across the living room, and balloons full of propane go up in flames in the backyard, so this new event did seem a bit tame. I spotted my father hovering near a huge bowl of tamales, waved him over, and suggested that we get a new act in motion for the laymen in the crowd: "I think they're hoping to see something explode."

"Yeah," he said through a mouthful of pork and cornmeal, "I'd say it's about time for the liquid nitrogen."

From behind the Christmas tree, my father produced a vat of super-subfreezing liquid, a common light bulb, and a half-dozen safety goggles. While the next contestant in the Shootout stationed himself at the keyboard, Dr. Bland plugged in some wires, handed out the glasses, and prepared to lower the glowing bulb into the steaming pot. "This," he said, "is what happens when three thousand Fahrenheit meets seventy-seven kelvin! Fire in the hole!"

The bulb dropped, and the crowd collectively held its breath—but nothing happened. The light bulb remained lit for three seconds in the vat, then fizzled. Dr. Bland furrowed his brow like a man immersed in thought; synapses in his brain fired and sent off electrical currents this way and that to retrieve notes and textbooks from the cerebral shelves, to check the facts and figures related to the matter, to try to understand what had—or had not—happened.

But the semester was over, and it didn't really matter. He shrugged and grabbed a carrot from a nearby vegetable platter. I saw what was coming—the Liquid Nitrogen Smash-Out, a foolproof, tested-and-true crowd-pleaser. He dunked the carrot for ten seconds and then shattered it like glass over the coffee table. "Anyone else want to try?" he asked as he set the bubbling vat on the floor.

Everyone did, of course, and frozen shrapnel began to fly. When the vegetables ran out, the participants went for napkins, tamale husks, flowers from the vase, and branches from the Christmas tree. Almost everything except fingers became fodder for the smashing, and the carpet was soon littered with debris.

It has long been a tradition at the Physics and Astronomy Party to plug wires into a dill pickle and set it aglow. It's a simple trick that takes place on the back-deck table, and at this year's gathering, a student was given the job of sinking the wires into either end of the vegetable. "The tough part," my father joked, "is not to get electrocuted." The young lady set down her beer, securely lodged the wires, then plugged in the cord. The pickle turned an alien yellow, began to hum like a spaceship, and started cooking from the inside out. For thirty minutes, the students played this game, laughing and rearranging the wires, adding more pickles, pouring beer over them, and somehow managing not to fry one another.

In the living room, an astronomy professor took his place in the Equation-Editing Shootout, but it was nearing Saturday morning by now, and few were watching. Wine and beer had numbed senses, and even the most respectable Ph.D.s had taken to sipping liquid nitrogen and then gargling it like mouthwash. They giggled and cheered as clouds of vapour blasted from their mouths. Bystanders covered their eyes, fearing that someone's tongue would crack and fall off, but there were no such accidents.

Actually, surprisingly, no one has ever filed an official complaint over the Physics and Astronomy Party. Like an experienced rock band, my father and his colleagues know how to put on a show *and* keep things in order.

But one incident from four years ago deserves mention. After a long and happy night, Dad and company goaded me into dumping a gallon of liquid nitrogen onto a hot barbecue. A violent mushroom cloud of burning ash enveloped me while twenty drunken guests went diving over chairs and tumbling into the doorway for shelter. The insulated vat dropped from my hands and shattered while I fell backward. I bumped my head on the wall, landed on shards of glass, and was temporarily blinded by dust. I might have had grounds for a lawsuit, but even in America, a fellow can't sue his parents and still expect a room to stay in.

This year, it had been my level-headed father's plan to ignite rocket fuel on the back porch as the grand finale, but only one of the required ingredients—pressurized nitrous oxide purchased from a novelty shop in the Castro—had been located. "We won't be going to the moon tonight," my father apologized to the half-dozen remaining students, "but this stuff will still burn." He lit up a blowtorch while a student opened an N_2O cartridge and filled a large red balloon with the gas. One student forced the nitrous oxide through a length of PVC piping while another ignited the gas on its way out the opposite end. It was true, nobody went to the moon; but the gas flared brilliantly like a miniature space shuttle for several seconds.

"This guy's so rad," a student said quietly to me. "He's such a cool professor."

"I know," I told him. "He's my dad."

The Tenses
of Landscape

RACKSTRAW DOWNES

Introduced by Michael Helm

As I go about the world I see things (people; their looks and feelings and thoughts; the things their thoughts have made, and the things that neither they nor their thoughts had anything to do with making; the whole range of the world) that, I cannot help feeling, Piero della Francesca or Bruegel or Goya or Cézanne would paint if they were here now—could not resist painting. Then I say to my wife, sadly: "What a pity we didn't live in an age when painters were still interested in the world!" . . . Man and the world are all that they ever were—their attractions are, in the end, irresistible; the painter will not hold out against them long.

— Randall Jarrell, "Against Abstract Expressionism"

Jarrell's prediction was not so bold, really; in matters of art or poetry, he never confused a development with a progression. But although the "attractions" of the world, both its history and outward forms, did in fact come to reassert themselves in painting, a half century later, we might not say so confidently that the world is all it ever was. If nothing else, we see it differently, or perhaps fail to see it for reasons that the poets, critics, and painters of the mid-twentieth century wouldn't have imagined. The sheer volume of images in it has changed its texture, and as a term, "art" itself has become nearly meaningless in its spreading democracy. As the technologies of image-making and reproduction have changed not just the depiction, but the subject—and not just the world, but our very faculties for appre-hending it—we're again likely to feel the need of what Jarrell called "the painter's praise."

In 1957, the same year that Jarrell's essay appeared, seventeen-year-old Rackstraw Downes left England for the United States to make the unlikely transition from a Cambridge English degree to (via the Hotchkiss School) a Yale M. F. A. in painting, with a specialty in geometric expressionism. A second great transition soon followed. Upon graduation, he moved to Maine and found there landscapes that we can suppose were something like those of his native Kent, which is to say compelling but not sublime beyond the human scale. In what might be viewed as a kind of return to origins (though the thought seems too neat, and Downes's art includes a practice of avoiding appealing falsehoods and easy parallels), what he discovered over the next few years seems to have been not just an unusual talent for realist painting, but a manner of approaching subjects that allowed him an intellectual engagement with the world as it is and its representation.

How to describe Downes's paintings? The subjects in a recent show at the Betty Cuningham Gallery in New York included scenes from New York City and its nearby parks, Staten Island's Snug Harbor, and power and water projects in the Texas desert. Many are public but unpeopled: the parks and theatre interiors; some present us the hidden spaces within public places: studies of wooden ducts in different light in the attic of the Snug Harbor Music Hall, and of the metal ducts below it. Without human figures but full of human artefacts, the paintings are almost anthropological.

One of the most interesting qualities of the work is how it coheres. Thematically, for example, the Texas paintings of electrical substations are of a piece with the retaining walls of a flood plain, but formally, they seem more conversant with the backstops of New York baseball parks or, from earlier drawings, the nettings of a driving range.

The show's mix of urban and rural emphasized within given paintings the ways in which the human meets the humanless (or "natural," though for a fuller reading of "nature," see Downes's essay). Note the many empty or elusive foregrounds, or the vegetable margins in the bursting *Cotton Club from Under the Viaduct at Riverside Drive and St. Clair Place 2003*, and compare this somewhat marvelling look at sheer human construction to the lone, unprepossessing building in mid-frame of the desert landscape in *Water-Flow Monitoring Installations on the Rio Grande near Presidio, Texas, 2002–2003 (5 parts. Part 1: Facing South, The Gauge Shelter, 1:30 P.M.)*, with its little hut that the eye would pass by as nondescript if it weren't so presently described.

The sheer skill of such work has a kind of unassailable authority. The paintings could hardly be more exact, but the exactness is to an actuality beyond what we can photograph or even see. The curved horizons in Downes's paintings are truer than the ones we perceive after our brains straighten them out for us—this effect, known as the "constancy principle," creates a reassuring but false sense of stability—and this counter-corrective aspect of Downes's paintings exposes one of the ways in which we lie to ourselves. In the same spirit, they are also slyly political at times: what are the consequences of all this heedless activity? we might ask.

In a recent article on Downes in *The New Yorker*, Peter Schjeldahl describes him as "a realist esteemed by people, including me, who normally have scant use for realism in art." He should also be esteemed as one of those rare painters who write with eloquence and scope about what they do. His magazine articles, introductions, published lectures, and small book of three essays, *In Relation to the Whole*, reveal a writer capable of discussing art and literature as if they belong to the same language. The writings remind us that even paintings that derive some of their power from wordlessness exist in contexts that are both historical and contemporary, both visual and conceptual. As Guy Davenport puts it in his essay on Paul Cadmus, "We have scant critical skills in . . . conflating a painter's thought with our literature and philosophy . . . The result is that we talk aesthetics and the politics of fashion and remain in dismal ignorance of meaning in some of the most interesting painting in all of history." In his writings, Downes has given us some ways of thinking about painting, and his painting, and the writers and thinkers who influence his attentions.

Every so often, excellence has its moment. Although Downes has been in steep ascendance for most of his painting life, his work has become especially necessary in the new century. The writings open up the paintings, and the paintings change the way we see, moment to moment. In this realist art of the mundane, loss and even violence is registered not in broken forms or perspectives, but as a creeping deficit in our perception of the ordinary. We're aware of the deficit only when the ordinary is restored to us in its infinite abundance.

THE TENSES OF LANDSCAPE

The earth, in fact, was a stretch of time.
— Laura Riding

I was born and raised in England and I think this has something to do with my attitude toward landscape. I don't have what I perceive as a New World sense of an antithesis between unspoiled nature and human culture; a landscape to me is a place where people live and work. There really was no wild nature in the South of England where I grew up and in Europe, as George Orwell said, "Every step you take you're probably treading on ten dead people." Already by the first century CE, a great proportion of Europe was penetrated by Roman roads. Whereas local roads tended to follow irregular courses that yielded to the physical characteristics of the terrain, the Romans preferred to build their roads in straight lines expressing a will to dominate and manipulate the landscape for human convenience and control. This will was expressed in other things the Romans did. The eroded hillsides of Calabria and Basilicata, which to this day support only a rather feeble growth of stunted trees, are the result of the drastic clear-cutting the Romans practiced in order to heat their immense bathhouses.

The Campagna around Rome itself once consisted of stable small farms worked by peasants practising a sustainable agriculture; i.e., raising a variety of crops and livestock. When the inhabitants left these farms in large numbers to fill the huge military drafts that took place during the Punic Wars, the countryside was taken over by land barons who practised intensive monoculture, often with prisoner-of-war labour. The soil was quickly exhausted by this type of farming; the land was consequently abandoned, and turned into malarial swamp. It still has—at least when I was last there—the feeling of a ghostly wasteland dotted with masonry, the scabs of antiquity hanging on.

We commonly sense a difference between various kinds of human intervention in the landscape though, and in fact, the cultures that built the megaliths at Stonehenge or Carnac, or cut the huge white men and horses into the chalk hills of southern England, do not seem to us exploitative or destructive in their physical impact on the landscape compared with the Romans. Nonetheless, our culture generally applauds Roman engineering, along with the engineering of our own time, as achievements in the name of progress, a word beloved by the proponents of the Industrial Revolution, who considered that their inventions would improve the lot of mankind, making us all more comfortable and happier. They thought of their tremendous engineering feats as the first of their kind since the ancient cultures of Egypt, Babylon, and Rome, and they applied a historicizing architectural ornamentation to these modern constructions that was meant to evoke that comparison. But with each step forward in the name of progress we seem to feel that there has been an attendant loss, and it often seems to be the role of landscape imagery to express or assuage this feeling. It is a role assumed

by some of the great masters of European landscape painting. In contrast to Dutch seventeenth-century landscape painters, who tend to express great optimism about the expanding agriculture and manufacturing of a newly independent state, Constable, stylistically innovative, is deeply retrospective in his landscape sensibility at a time of drastic changes and social unrest in the English countryside. Also, things that must have once seemed like interpolations in the landscape become, to later generations, the very thing they feel they are losing, have lost, or wish they had. Claude Lorraine used the triumphs of Roman engineering to help him image a timeless world where man's ambition seems both magnificent and reconciled with nature; while in Corot's work, Roman ruins have become organic parts of the landscape. Here we are dealing with a question of assimilation that is both mental (we get used to things) and physical (they decay).

The issue of loss seems a particularly sensitive one in the North American situation, because when the Europeans came here they found nature in a peculiarly abundant and pristine state compared with what they had left behind. The accounts by early explorers of the flora and fauna they found are almost ecstatic. In the nineteenth century the French etcher, Rodolphe Bresdin, made a pilgrimage here to find what he thought he could find nowhere else, virgin forests. Even today some bits of these survive. But I don't think "virgin nature" is an adequate description of what the Europeans found. I think they found human societies that were not interested in a progressive notion of culture but in a cyclical idea of life. Even what Europeans have taken to be one of the most (in our own terms) "advanced" forms of New World culture, the Mayan calendar, is a cyclical account of time. Nature in these cyclical societies is not something for people to overcome, because it is not something separate: people are part of it. At the first Earth Day in 1970, I remember a Native American speaker saying, "If the white man does not respect his mother the earth and his father the sun, he will not endure." This did not sound gratuitous, it did not sound like hyperbole. But even though our progressive society has come to acknowledge the truths that are expressed by cyclical societies, I don't see any vigorous attempts to incorporate these truths into our physical lives. Our biologists deplore the loss of biodiversity, but progressive societies have almost completely eradicated any surviving cyclical ones whose mode of existence fosters that diversity. Our present fascination with virtual reality and information networks demonstrates that we really don't believe E. M. Forster's forebodings about the dystopian technological nightmare depicted in his novella *The Machine Stops*, where physical reality has been almost abolished and all that remains is comfort and ideas. That nightmare is our new playground. One of the few movements that seriously and effectively backs off from our progressive culture is the or-

ganic gardening and farming movement, which began to grow and take on significance in response to the sort of revelations about what is happening to the environment contained in Rachel Carson's *Silent Spring*. To me the interest of this movement is less in its effort to put food on the market that is healthier for humans, than in its intent to take plentiful crops off the land and at the same time leave that land in better condition than the farmer found it; to use no substances in this process that would be toxic to any life in the environment, and to create no waste products that cannot be absorbed back into the farming process. This is not an agriculture that expresses a desire to return to something lost, it is a hopeful agriculture that expresses faith in the future.

So I would concur with the philosopher Edmund Leites in seeing a lot of ambivalence in the overall picture of our attitude to the relationship between progress and nature. We may yearn for a past, real or fictional, but we go forward anyway. Here is a contradiction involving time. We create nature reservations, while living somewhere where nature is largely excluded or, as we think, under control. Here is a contradiction involving space. In another spatial contradiction we try to hide the price of progress from ourselves, to turn our backs on it, a point made by Ann Bermingham in her

book *Landscape and Ideology*, where she tells of a development in the early years of the Industrial Revolution: while the factory owners of the late eighteenth century like Josiah Wedgwood lived at their factories, later owners, as the factories got grimmer, moved away, lived elsewhere. This trend continues in our own time, where we take the profits from a polluted industrial park and spend them buying a cottage by an unspoiled stream. When I choose images for my paintings, I'm especially attracted to sites that bring together separated realities like these, realities that are really functions of one another, and that we need to connect again in order to see holistically what we are doing. For instance, the painting *U.S. Scrap Metal Gets Shipped For Reprocessing in Southeast Asia, Jersey City*, 1994, represents a cove on New York Harbor, just south of the Statue of Liberty. To the left of centre is a new condominium development built on an old pier, and expressing both by its architecture (a sort of Sheetrock-Château style) and its name (Port Liberté) a certain social pretension. The condo residents like living here because there's a direct ferry to the financial district of New York, where many of them work (you can see the World Trade Center on the far left of the painting), and where electronic transactions of an extraordinary degree of abstraction take place. An example of the concrete

physical results of such transactions is happening right across the cove from the condo (on the right-hand side of the painting) where scrap metal is being sorted, baled, and loaded into barges that are then pulled out to deep water and reloaded onto ocean-going ships that carry it to Southeast Asia; there it will be made into Hondas and transistors, and shipped back to us. In the middle of the cove is a sign of the decay of industrial life, rotting supports for a pier that once carried an oil pipeline connecting tankers in the deep water to the refineries on shore. Around the cove marsh grasses flourish in the interstitial areas we haven't yet found a use for. Canada geese congregate on warm sandy banks exposed by the low tide, and egrets feed in the shallows in front of the barges.

In The High Island Oil Field, February, After the Passage of a Cold Front, 1990, depicts an oil field, long past its prime, on the Texas coast. It represented for me an accommodation, a sort of peaceable kingdom. The pumps are on raised platforms because this land, which is at sea level, floods during a hurricane. Cows, horses, and wading birds share this 1,200-acre field with the pumps, and when strong winds blow in from the north after the passage of a cold front, the sediments that are pumped up with the oil and natural gas and that collect in the bottoms of ditches, are stirred up so

the ditch water looks red. The perspective down the centre of this painting is the raised embankment of an old railroad bed. The cows like to congregate and lie down to rest on this long-infertile ground because it dries off quickly after a rain; and so they dung it up intensively too. So, it is gradually beginning to regain fertility and support a sparse cover of weeds, which spread in by runners from either side of the embankment. Here the tenses of a landscape imagery that represents what is lost or threatened are reversed; we see decaying industrialization being replaced or reclaimed by the progress of nature. These weeds interest me more than ancient redwoods; they are the vanguard of nature's forces as she wages *her* war back on us; or perhaps I should say, here nature re-embraces us, her prodigal sons and daughters. These weeds give the idea of nature not as a state we've lost but as a process with a future.

My paintings are executed from start to finish on site in the landscape and take months. When you work outdoors, you surrender a lot of control over your subject and that is what I like about it, the interactive, experiential character of it. It is the opposite of starting with a clear-cut idea and projecting that into the work. You learn about the site as you proceed; no matter what thoughts or opinions I may have about what is there when I begin, what comes to concern me as I work are the things themselves, not any sense I make of them. I made an oil sketch one April in response to the huge scale of a scrap metal pile towering over the fence in front of it. When I returned to the site with a large canvas made to proportions that would give me room for those two leading players, the pile was gone, sold to

the Japanese. Did that mean I no longer had a subject? Well, no: it meant I followed what was *now* actually offered at the site (*A Fence at the Periphery of a Jersey City Scrap-Metal Yard*, 1993). The ground, bare in spring, produced a fine crop of weeds as summer wore on, and the fence became a subject in itself; perforated by tiny holes that let the wind through, it allowed you to sense mysteriously the semi-visible operations going on inside it. So, working from nature is not a technical issue; it has to do with letting the realities of the outside world impinge on and steer the activities of your own artistic world.

I've talked a lot about *imagery*. This term, like its sibling *narrative*, is almost unavoidable in aesthetic discussions today. That's okay, provided we recognize them for what they are: x-ray terms. They look through or past the artwork's body. But in art it is often the body more than the imagery that really signifies. In his essay about Swift's *Gulliver's Travels* called "Politics vs. Literature," George Orwell deals with the role of imagery or narrative in works of art, and the question of our endorsing, or not, the point of view expressed by them. He says *Gulliver's Travels* has always been one of his favourite books, he's read it eight or ten times, and he believes his taste in this is not aberrant because the book has never been out of print since its first publication and has been translated into some twenty languages. But, he says, the point of view of this book, its attitude to life, could not be more antithetical to his own. He hates its know-nothing attitude to science and knowledge, its disgust with the human body, its belief in an over-organized state based on a kind of slave population. So how can he love it? In his answer he does not praise its formal beauties; he says, rather, that the point of view it represents is something that is a component, even though only a small or partial one, of what we all feel, sometimes. There are days when any of us might wake up having thoughts like that about life. I would extrapolate from this and say that nothing could be more disappointing to me than to go to a show and find that it contained nothing but works expressing a point of view about landscape similar to my own; and that art moves us when the point of view, no matter what that is—provided, as Orwell says, it is not insane—is strongly, finely, richly, subtly, poignantly, or in whatever way, embodied in the piece.

Is there really an opposition between nature and progress? For me, the answer is partly real, partly linguistic. I find I use the word *nature* in two ways. One is as used by Schiller in his essay "Naive and Sentimental Poetry," 1795, who speaks of nature as meaning "plants, minerals, animals and landscapes, as well as human nature in children, in the customs of country folk, and the primitive world . . . Nature, considered in this wise, is for us nothing but the voluntary presence, the subsistence of things on their own, their existence in accordance with their own immutable laws." I take *voluntary* to mean "not through the agency of humans." Then there is the sense used by Buckminster Fuller, quoted by the poet Gary Lenhart as saying, "If it isn't nature, it doesn't exist." Here nature means everything that exists physically, since everything is subject to the laws of nature, including man's inventions.

Since the practice of the simplest forms of agriculture (e.g., burning underbrush to improve forest hunting grounds), mankind has tried to improve its environment, as beavers dam streams. We are experimental creatures working within the laws of nature. Our inventions that backfire, such as the Aswan Dam or CFCs, are experiments that do not work successfully within those laws. The fact that we can neutralize our stockpiles of CFCs by using a substance found in rhubarb indicates the ongoing interaction between Schiller's and Fuller's natures. If we smile with pleasure at this solution, we reveal the value we put on Schiller's nature, and acknowledge a distinction between different kinds of "everything that exists physically." With this distinction we chide ourselves for our narcissistic preoccupation with those things we made ourselves over those things we didn't.

Progress is an evaluation of change. As technological change, the Aswan Dam or CFCs are problematic; not progress, just change. But the term *progress* has come to be most commonly used in a propaganda sense, to endorse change, to sell it as inevitable. The distinction between change that is harmful and change that is not gets obliterated, and a suspicion of, or antipathy to change develops, replacing a prudently experimental attitude.

Schiller's nature, consisting of so many things we would never have conceived of inventing as well as things we find useful to us, remains a deep source of wonder. As such, even if it does not answer the question, What are we here for?, it nonetheless obviates the necessity of asking it.

The Casual Moment

AMIT CHAUDHURI

I always find it a bit surprising when I hear the directors and producers of Hindi films say, "This one is very good—it's almost as good as Hollywood." I realize it's probably a quality of professionalism, a technical finesse, they have in mind; because, creatively, mainstream Hollywood cinema today is arguably the least interesting and most infantile cinema being made anywhere. Its success might be an object of emulation—but does it compel admiration in any other sense?

For ever since we can remember, Hollywood has been not only a principal producer, but also the chief definition of popular cinema. But, in the last twenty years or so, it has become more: it has become, almost unobtrusively, a universal type. I feel this especially when I am in the DVD and video section of a book or music shop in Britain—there is cinema, and then, in a corner, there is "world" cinema. What's happened to the adjective "world" here is striking: robbed, both physically and conceptually, of size, volume, and mastery, of the glamour it possesses in other conjunctions ("world famous," "world class"), it has become a ghost of itself, an uncharacteristically minor term. The "world" is an obscure and down-at-the-heel Hollywood suburb, which people, these days, visit infrequently.

The transformation of Hollywood into a universal has been appropriate to its role in the unipolar world, as a sort of statist art form in an age in which states are disappearing; but it has cost it artistically. When I say "artistic," I have a particular notion of the word in mind, a notion that was fully expressed only by twentieth-century modernism and its various tributaries, but which has been at work in the domain of art across time and cultures: the idea that the "universal" in art is in constant tension with the particular, the random, the aleatory.

In an intriguing essay, "The Sacred Circulation of National Images," the social scientist Partha Chatterjee is puzzled and engrossed by what has happened to these "national images"—for instance, the Taj Mahal; Shah Jahan's Red Fort—as they've been represented in our textbooks in the last forty or fifty years; that is, in India's relatively brief, but palpably long, history as a republic.

Chatterjee discovers that early photographs and engravings found in textbooks dating back, say, to the twenties, are gradually replaced in textbooks after 1947 by a certain kind of line drawing. He finds no economic raison d'être for this change: "Are they cheaper to print? Not really; both are printed from zinc blocks made by the same photographic process." But the more telling change occurs in the nature of the representations themselves, as the pictures of certain monuments are transformed into "national icons." The earlier pictures and photos, Chatterjee finds, have an element of the random in their composition—an engraving of the Taj Mahal has a nameless itinerant before it; an early photograph shows a scattering of "native" visitors before the same building; early pictures of the Red Fort or the *ghats* in Benares have the same sort of "redundant" detail in the foreground.

As these monuments are turned into "national icons" in post-independence history textbooks, the pictures are emptied of signs of randomness, emptied, indeed, of all but the monument itself, and a new credo and economy of representation comes into existence: "There must be no hint of the picturesque or the painterly, no tricks of the camera

angle, no staging of the unexpected or the exotic. The image must also be shorn of all redundancy . . ." Although Chatterjee places this "emptying" of the textbook image in the context of the Indian nation-state, and identifies this as a process by which national monuments are turned into "sacred" images, its impetus seems as much Platonic as nationalist: a nostalgia for the ideal likeness, unvitiated by reality's unpredictability. Something similar has happened to Hollywood in the last twenty-five years: an iconization has taken place; in the meantime, the aleatory has been steadily suppressed. If you study a frame in a contemporary Hollywood movie, you note how it has been denuded of the random, the redundant, of what Barthes, looking at stills from Eisenstein, called the irreducible "third meaning"; even the incidental details—a stall selling newspapers or fruit on a street—are a premeditated part of the design. This is the transformation of Hollywood from art or entertainment into, to borrow a phrase from Chatterjee, a "sacred circulation of images" in our globalized present; from cinema to a Platonic likeness of cinema ("true-blue cinema," to quote a film critic in *The Telegraph* in a review of the film *Black*); and more. What is revealing is how easily people have accepted this sacralization, and how few have remarked on the passing of the random from "true-blue cinema."

As a reader (and writer) who has a particular investment in the occurrence of the redundant and the random in works of art, I find revealing the disappearance of these elements from some of the major art forms in the world we now live in.

"Much of the best things in a [John] Ford film," said his devotee, Satyajit Ray, after Ford's death in 1973, "has the mysterious, indefinable quality of poetry. Because some of them appear casual—even accidental—it is difficult to realize how much experience and mastery lie behind them."

And then he provides an instance, a "moment," from the Ford film *Fort Apache*. "Two men stand talking on the edge of a deep ravine. There is a broken bottle lying alongside. One man gives it a casual kick and sends it flying over the edge. A few seconds later, in a gap in the conversation, the soundtrack registers the faintest of clinks. That's all. This is the sort of thing that belongs uniquely to the cinema. What it does is to invest a casual moment with poetic significance. Those who look for 'meaning' here, whether symbolic or literary, and are disappointed not to find it, are obviously unaware of what makes for poetry in the cinema."

Ray's description here is itself composed in the language of the aleatory—"accidental"; "faintest"; "that's all"; the repetition, three times, of "casual." The elegy for Ford is an elegy for a certain kind of sensibility that cinema—even mainstream Hollywood cinema—once accommodated, for Ford was a commercial filmmaker. Like the person who, in the twenties, made the engraving of the Taj Mahal with the single itinerant before it, Ford, by his own admission, was doing a "job." Ray begins his tribute with a speculation—"either Ford did not think of himself as an artist," or, as Ray believes, he possessed such confidence in his mastery that he didn't worry about the pedestrian commissions he sometimes took up. One might wonder, similarly, about the person who made that early engraving. On the one hand, it's just another textbook picture; on the other, it's lit with the instinct for the casual that makes it unrepeatable.

The Fruits of War

LEILAH NADIR

Iraq is in me, although I have not been in Iraq. The closest I have been is Deir Ezzor, Syria, a nondescript town on the Iraqi border. In 1992 I visited Deir Ezzor to renew my Syrian visa. There, in the middle of a gritty desert the townspeople speak Arabic with an Iraqi accent and listen to Iraqi music. So even in the Middle East, there are Iraqis who, like me, don't live in Iraq. Internationally, there are around five million exiles from a country of twenty-five million; about one-fifth of Iraqis don't live in Iraq.

Just after the Gulf War, I was too afraid to go to Baghdad to visit my relatives. I didn't know what the impact of a North American visitor would have been on my family. The Ba'athist regime was known for killing or imprisoning people they thought might be their enemies, and having a foreigner in your house could put you under suspicion. I also didn't know what impact a war-torn country and family would have on me. But I yearned to go. My independent travels in the Middle East skirted the country, through Turkey, Syria, and Jordan.

Until the Gulf War, I hadn't thought much of my father being Iraqi, and I hadn't thought much of my mother being English. Born in Baghdad, my father was educated by the Jesuits at Baghdad College and grew up in a westernized household. Though he remembers various revolutions and political upheavals, his childhood was happy and comfortable. The family vacationed in Beirut and Safita, Syria. His father loved to travel, read, and discuss philosophy and theology. In 1960, at sixteen, my father left Iraq on an engineering scholarship to attend a college in northern England, fell in love, married my mother, and moved to Canada in the late sixties. He has never been back to Iraq.

We moved back to England in 1974, when I was three. During my childhood, I saw my Iraqi grandparents, aunts, great-aunts, and uncles when they drove from Iraq across Europe to

London. Iraqis like to travel in big family groups, and my family loved travelling through Europe and visiting Rome and Paris before crossing the channel to London. The political terrors of the eighties and nineties eventually affected my family's ability to travel, but by 1982, we had moved back to Canada, and I didn't expect to see my Iraqi relatives often. But I always thought that I would see them again someday. Iraq, for me, was my family, my father, hearing Arabic conversation peppered with English, eating Arabic food, and listening to Arabic music.

I was a university student when the Persian Gulf War started in 1991. Like most of the world, I believed in the guilt of Saddam Hussein's regime in invading Kuwait. I was a spectator at a protest die-in against the war on the steps of the Arts Building at McGill University. An air-raid signal sounded and students fell on the steps playing dead. I was moved for the innocent Iraqis they represented, until I heard a scream from an upstairs window. It was a Kuwaiti student screaming that his family was in Kuwait, that we had no idea what war was like, and how dared we protest the war.

From the beginning of that first Gulf war until the collapse of Saddam Hussein's regime in 2003, I had no contact with my grandparents or other relatives in Iraq. One year to the day after the September 11 attacks, an Iraqi Canadian friend, Miriam (not her real name; we all still fear reprisals, so most names in this essay have been changed), flew in defiance of that fear from Vancouver to Amman and from there took a bus to Baghdad. As a photo-

journalist, she wanted to document the end of Saddam Hussein's regime and see how members of her extended family were living through the buildup to war. She had been to Iraq before with international groups that protested the sanctions. She promised her friends and family that she would come back home if a war began.

_____

My father had never spoken much about Iraq. I asked him if he thought that Iraqis would be happy to see Saddam removed. He said, "No one hates Saddam as much as I do. But this war is wrong. It would be seen in the Middle East as an unprovoked invasion by the West, confirming everyone's worst fears about Western imperialism."

At the time, I believed that protests might delay the war. I began writing letters to politicians, sending articles to my friends, speaking out, and going to peace vigils. The first protest my engineer father had attended in his entire life was against the war. "I can't believe I'm protesting for saving Saddam. It's ridiculous," he said, but he marched anyway. My Iraqi relatives in London said, "How can he have weapons? The country has nothing, never mind weapons."

I called Miriam at her hotel in Baghdad. She told me she had fallen in love with a man from "the country beside your country," and I knew immediately that she thought her phone was being tapped and did not want to risk even saying the word _America_. I kept asking her if she would leave if war broke out, but we both knew it was too late. There were reports of the borders being closed, as neighbouring countries did not want floods of refugees pouring out of Iraq. "No one is leaving Baghdad," Miriam said. "Except journalists."

My family spoke to our relatives in Baghdad before the war, but we were more frightened than they were. "We have lived through war before," they said. "We know what it is to be bombed. In a way, the bombing has never stopped."

My middle-class relatives in Baghdad were stockpiling their yearly rations of flour, sugar, and rice: one sack of each and a small amount of tea. "We are already dieting," my aunt tried to joke. No perishable items, of course, because the fridge and stove wouldn't work as soon as the electrical plant was bombed. The neighbours were digging a well. During the Gulf War, the water supply was hit immediately ("Why?" my aunt asked). But the well water was contaminated, and they'd have to boil it before they could drink it. They were planning to cook on a portable stove until their one canister of gas ran out. Then they would look out at the twenty Seville orange trees in the garden.

When my father lived in Iraq as a boy, the trees produced juicy oranges as bitter as lemons. "The juice was excellent for making many delicious dishes and salads," my aunt said on the telephone. "Your father and his cousins used to collect them and we'd keep the juice for the winter—a hundred jars of orange juice," she said, "and we'd make marmalade with the peel." During the Gulf War, the trees lost all their leaves. "Maybe it was the lack of water," she said, "or they were poisoned." After the Gulf War, the trees produced deformed fruit that was absolutely inedible. "The orange trees are dying." When the gas ran out, they planned to chop them down and burn them for fuel.

———————

The Persian Gulf War in 1991 had devastated my family. When war broke out, my father's cousin had just graduated from university. The very next day, without any army training, he was sent to the front. He was the kind of gracious young man whom everyone wants in their family. He'd be the first to put up a curtain rail, fetch watermelons from the market, or fix the roof. He was killed on the first day of the war. His body was brought back to the house in a cardboard coffin on the roof of a car. His father, my father's uncle, dropped dead of a heart attack three days later.

War doesn't leave even the dead in peace. My grandmother was buried in the beautiful old Assyrian Catholic church in the centre of Baghdad, the place where my father took his first communion. My grandfather created a headstone engraved with calligraphic writing to mark her burial place. During the Gulf War, the church was destroyed. Not by a direct attack, but by the reverberations of the incessant bombing nearby. The walls began to crumble. The priest summoned my great-aunt and asked her to move my grandmother's remains. She still cries when she tells this story.

The pictures that started to come out of Iraq, as the war began in March 2003, were the first direct images I had seen of the country in years. Thin Iraqi men (who looked like my father) with their arms in the air; Iraqi men hooded and bound with plastic cuffs, one with a child sitting beside him; and the unforgettable photographs of the boy, Ali, who lost his arms and parents to the war.

A few days after "liberation," when the rampant looting and burning of the National Museum and the National Archives took place, we got a call from our cousin Karim on a satellite phone in Baghdad. He said that everyone had survived the war. The call cost him ten dollars for one minute, and then he was gone.

It wasn't until June 2003, two months after the war had "ended," that we heard from Karim again. He had an e-mail address, and miraculously, the computer at his office still worked. The phone line was one of the only ones working in central Baghdad. I decided to send him an e-mail. I can tell you that Karim is married, a father of two, a Christian, a professional, and in his mid-forties. I had never met or talked to him before.

Karim was so happy for us to be in touch: "This is one of the benefits of war. They say that calamity

will combine a nation!" He asked me if I knew Arabic, and I had to admit that I didn't and blamed it quickly on my father. "You should speak Arabic, you are Iraqi. You must learn!" I promised him I would. I asked him what he thought of the war, and he said that of course he felt very differently from me. He told me that he had survived three wars spanning nearly twenty years, and that "there is no one that we did not fight."

"We spent most of our life in conscription in the army," he said. He was supposed to do twenty months of mandatory service. As a result of "the continuous wars," he spent over seventy months in the army, but still less time than many of his friends. "All the Iraqi people were looking to this war to bring the end of a tyrannical regime," he said. Most people didn't make preparations, just stockpiled food and water. He didn't even do that, as he thought the war would be quick, knowing what he knew about the Iraqi army.

The war took twenty days and they were the most miserable days of his life. He could see the airplanes and cruise missiles flying over his head, and everyone expected the bombs would fall on their houses. "The explosions made a terrifying noise and each time we said that the house would fall down, and the doors and windows shook as if they would explode."

One night, the British and American forces attacked at ten in the evening and didn't stop until ten the next morning. "Twelve hours, and you might not believe it, but they did not stop for a moment." His wife and twelve-year-old daughter could not stop shaking, "even though I gave my wife tablets." At first, they thought it was an earthquake because the house moved: "I felt the tiles on the ground would jump in my face." They were standing beside the walls and could not move, even for a drink of water, for twelve hours. "It is difficult, I know, for you to believe, but it is the truth. The Americans said that it was a clean war, but it was the dirtiest war for civilians."

At the beginning of the war, they had water, electricity, and communication. Then after a week, they heard on the news that the American communication companies were complaining because these centres had not been attacked, and this was part of the deal. Then the forces did destroy all the power plants and communication centres. "So we lost electricity and lived in darkness. And we lost each other without the telephone, and then the explosions at night were even more terrifying." I kept thinking of my great-aunt Lina, living alone in the dark as the bombs fell night after night, with not even the phone for company.

It was difficult for Karim to e-mail me for several days, and when he finally did, he told me that they had not had any electricity or water for twenty-five days. None. I mentally unplugged everything that needed electricity or water in my apartment; it would be like stopping blood flowing in the veins of the house. And yet, in the next sentence, he was saying that he thought it was wonderful that I was a writer, but he would prefer that, as a young woman, I would "choose to write romantic stories, not sad ones."

He described the shock of the Americans entering Baghdad. No one had expected to see tanks in the streets. "Now I must tell you a terrible story that happened to my friend's daughter and her family on that same day." The family was at her husband's parents' house when they decided to return to their own house near the centre of Baghdad. She drove with her husband and their children, two boys and one daughter. "Suddenly they saw an American tank up the road, and without warning, the tank began to shoot at the car with the huge tank machine gun. Instantly, the father and the three children were killed. My friend's daughter survived and leapt out of the car, waving at the soldiers to stop." The soldiers started shooting at her. "She ran through the shooting and found a house. It was a miracle she survived. She was taken back to her father's house. Her clothes were full of blood. She was like someone who had lost her mind."

A few days later, her brothers went to the place where the catastrophe had taken place, but the Americans threw them out. After five days, they were allowed to take the bodies, which the Americans had buried quickly using only a shovel to dig the graves. "When her brothers asked the Americans, 'Why did you kill this family?' the answer was simple: 'We are sorry, it was an accident.'"

Miriam had stayed with her Iraqi family throughout the war, against her parents' wishes. She was selling photographs to all kinds of international media and especially *The New York Times*. As she was still in Baghdad, I asked her if she would mind going to see Lina, who was looking after the house that my father grew up in, and to see Karim and his family. She agreed to go and take photographs.

On July 18, I opened my e-mail to a photograph of my great-aunt Lina sitting on a threadbare couch in the house in Baghdad where my father grew up. My friend wrote: "She was there alone when I arrived by taxi and hadn't been feeling well. There was no electricity and it was very hot without a fan. She was sitting in the dark. But she felt like getting out of the house." The photographs showed a woman who looked much older than seventy, but was unmistakably my great-aunt whom I had teased on holiday in Greece many years ago because she didn't know how to swim. My father said later, "She was a very tough lady. All the women in my family were strong and powerful. You know, she worked in Customs, very high up." Her eyes were intense and alive, but she looked angry. In her hand was a paper fan. The roots of her hair were grey, but she had obviously still been dying her hair red despite everything.

In the second photograph, she is driving my friend through the streets of Baghdad. Her arm is raised, hand flexed open, and she is obviously talking. These photographs were the first that my father and his sisters had seen of their aunt in thirteen years. Miriam said it was strange to walk into the house in the middle of Baghdad, so far from home, and see photographs of me and my family framed around the room.

As winter came to Vancouver, Karim gave me his office phone number in Baghdad. I was nervous about speaking to him. We had built up a level of intimacy in the e-mails, but we didn't know each other. I dialled the number and the line took about a minute to connect. The blank space of the quiet line gave me the feeling that Karim was beyond some barrier I could not cross. The line was muffled, and we had to keep repeating ourselves. I found that I was shouting into the phone. I was relieved by his laughter as he described the occupation of his country by the Americans. He told me that my great-aunt Lina had just had a back operation and that she couldn't walk, but her phone still didn't work so I couldn't call her. He has a friend who is an excellent doctor, so he got "a very low price," he laughed again. He said that the Iraqi police had finally been given good weapons and some authority by the Americans, that they were very brave and doing an excellent job. I told him that we were only hearing bad news about Iraq. "This is an old film; we have seen all of this before. The Americans want an excuse to stay here," he said. Then he added, "We all know that Saddam was an agent of America, and he has finally delivered Iraq to America."

Karim still couldn't believe that American soldiers were in the streets of Baghdad. "You see, for fifteen years we can't think about America. It was the enemy. We can't say the word *America*, we know nothing about America. It was completely banned, it didn't exist. No Iraqis were allowed to travel to other countries. We didn't have satellite television, most of the internet sites were 'Access Denied,' and our newspapers were controlled by Saddam. The world didn't know us, and we didn't know the world, especially America."

Now the streets teemed with American soldiers. "America is here in Baghdad. It walks in our

streets, eats at our restaurants, drinks tea at our cafés, buys goods in our markets. We like to sit in our garden at night, especially in the summer, and the American soldiers walk by and our children run up to them saying, 'Hello Americans! Hello!'"

In the summer, Karim felt sorry for the soldiers in Baghdad as the temperature was forty to forty-five degrees Celsius. "Their faces were so red, like tomatoes, and they had these small tanks on their backs and a little tube coming out and they were drinking water from it. Just drinking water all the time, but I don't think it helped them. They were still hot."

Iraq, a year after the war, was in a terrible limbo, a place without hope living on the brink of grief. When Saddam Hussein, hated by most Iraqis, was seen having his teeth examined like a wild creature, many Iraqis I know did not react with a howl of sweet revenge. They felt strangely sorry for him.

Saddam's humiliation symbolized the humiliation of Iraq.

––––––––––––

Karim e-mails me in June 2004, as his phone isn't working again. I ask him how he is, and he writes back, "Still alive." He explains that a few days previously, he had gone to the central bank on Al Rasheed Street in central Baghdad, and the next day, a huge bomb had exploded in the exact place where he had been standing. This was the second time this had happened to him in a week. "They're trying to get me," he jokes. I ask him if he believes in the elections and if they will work, and he says, wisely I think, "First we have to see whose names are on the ballot."

Karim tells me my great-aunt Lina's phone is finally working so I can call her. My heart beats wildly as the phone rings and rings. Finally she answers "Allo," as if she knows it is going to be me. Immediately she starts speaking in English, good English. I am shocked. "I can't walk well, because I have had my back operation." I realize that is why it took her a long time to get to the phone. We chat. We don't talk about the war. We don't talk about the occupation. We don't talk about the lack of electricity, money, or freedom. We talk about my love life. She wants to know when I am getting married and is worried that my younger sister is getting married before me. I laugh it off, but she is persistent. As I listen to her, my skin prickles, and I suddenly know what she smells like. I can feel her enfolding me in her soft, fleshy arms as she did when I was a child. I recognize the rasp in her throat as she speaks English with a guttural accent. She is so close, and the memories of the times when I saw her in Europe flood back. She is real, she has lived through all of this, and she is talking to me. I realize I have missed her. I ask her if I should come and visit. "In six months . . . come in six months." My father tells me afterwards that in Iraq, six months means never. It is a figure of speech, like saying "back in a second."

––––––––––––

Miriam finally came back safely from Baghdad with a gift for me. "I told the man selling antiques in the souk that I needed a present for an Iraqi girl who has never been to Baghdad, something to encourage her to come and visit." I opened the soft cloth and pulled out a silver jug with an elongated, curvaceous spout and Arabic calligraphy etched onto the front. Miriam didn't know what it was used for in Iraq, maybe a coffee pot or just a decorative object. It sits on my mantelpiece beside a silver plate that one of my mother's sisters brought back from Baghdad in the sixties and gave to me recently. I still don't know when I will go to Baghdad, even though I long to go. The silver still life whispers to me. Maybe in six months. . . .

A Late Response from Jane Porter

Dear Tarzan,

I have read your letter—your several letters—in the Winter
2004 *Brick* and have fallen frequently in love again, as the
marmoset falls for the baboon, as the mongoose longs for
the cobra. You have been all the men these letters promise.
I knew this when we shared our first vine together, in transit
from one tree to another, me dangling from your neck like
some voluptuous adornment. All trees looked the same to me
in those days, but thanks to you, I now know each by its jungle
name, and can speak to them as individuals. Sometimes they
tell me of your travels: to them you are "Quite the swinger,"
and I know they mean this as the highest praise.

You want me? You got me! Hunt for me, you mighty jungle
fighter. . . . I will be hiding in the underbrush near Penelope
the Tree. I miss you.

Devotedly,
Your Jane

Please remember to inflate your tires. A public service announcement from *Brick*.

Two Hemispheres

NADINE McINNIS

I first encountered the photographs of women patients of the Surrey County Lunatic Asylum as part of an exhibit on photography and science at the National Gallery of Canada in 1997. Almost lost amidst the dramatic images from space, the earliest x-rays, and playful art shots were nine small sepia figures framed together. They were very disturbing, despite their small stature. I carried them with me once I left the exhibit. They insinuated themselves into my unconscious so that one or another of their faces would drift up to the surface from time to time.

In 1997, I was in the midst of a decade of healthy years before the re-emergence of my own illness, major depression, in 2001. That long episode of suffering, and I can call it nothing else, lasted two years. It was during this time that the memory of the women's faces became more insistent. I thought long about how fragile the human mind can be and how these women might have experienced their illnesses before the age of pharmaceuticals, which, at that time, seemed to be causing me more grief than relief. They haunted me until I found a way to listen to them and connect my personal story to theirs in an exploration of the subjective experience of emotional and mental distress. In *Two Hemispheres*, the series of poems I wrote, I interspersed my imaginative engagement with these women's faces with the story of my family's and my own experiences of mental illness. I found that the more I looked at these women's faces, the less disturbing they became. Eventually, they seemed familiar, in all senses of the word.

Although there were other medical photographers in the 1850s in England, I was drawn to the photos taken by Dr. Hugh W. Diamond, Medical Superintendent of Women at the Surrey County Lunatic Asylum. Other photos, taken at Bethlem asylum, for instance, seem harsh, like mug shots exposing too much illness and not enough individuality. Dr. Diamond's photos are full-body poses, gently lit, allowing the subject's character to shine through. The patients seem remarkably open to the photographer. Some of them hold objects, whether an apple, a handiwork, or a pigeon, that must have personal significance to them. The subjects seem to be full participants in the photographic process instead of examples of illness.

The photographs must have been significant to these women patients as well. It's hard now to imagine how revolutionary photography would have seemed at the time. Paintings preserved the faces of the wealthy and influential, but photography was democratic, capturing the subtle facial expressions of even these indigent women who survive in image only. An essay published at the time by a visitor to the asylum describes how the photographs, hung in the ward for the most severe and volatile cases, had not been damaged in any way.

Dr. Diamond started his study of psychiatric patients in 1850, after the wet collodion process was developed. The new photographic process allowed an exposure time of seconds rather than up to ten minutes. This allowed him to photograph patients who, because of their illnesses, might have been unable to sit still (and in restraints) for the time required by previous techniques. His stated intentions were primarily scientific in nature. He was most interested in the way photography could provide objective categorization of mental illnesses. But what is obvious from the photographs is that Dr. Diamond was also a skilful photographer whose portraits are as insightful as they are beautiful. As

any artist must be, Dr. Diamond was open to mystery in a way many of his fellow scientists might not have been. As he writes in his 1856 article "On the Application of Photography to the Physiognomic and Mental Phenomena of Insanity": "The Photographer . . . needs in many cases no aid from any language of his own, but prefers rather to listen, with the picture before him, to the silent but telling language of nature."

The case notes for the patients have been lost. None of Dr. Diamond's notes or photographs survive in the Springfield Hospital (formerly the Surrey County Asylum) archives. What limited information that does exist can be found in an essay by Dr. John Conolly, published in 1858 in the *Medical Times and Gazette*. Dr. Conolly's focus is primarily on the physical expressions and features that indicate the nature of illness. Three of the women featured in Dr. Diamond's collection of photographs (only twenty or so of these photographs have survived) are discussed briefly in his essay, but only the most fleeting discussion of their history is included. Instead of working from these meagre facts to create realistic portraits in the poems that make up *Two Hemispheres*, I engaged with the women in the photographs directly and imaginatively.

While working on my series of poems, I was surprised to discover that I harboured misconceptions about the quality of psychiatric care available in mid-nineteenth-century England. The images of the mad woman in the attic, women chained and mistreated in dank, horrible captivity, or women imprisoned because of nonconformity to limited norms, were hard to shake for someone like me, whose creative teeth were cut on the feminist writing of the 1970s and 1980s. Abuses existed before the reforms of the mid-1800s, but after that time, there was a concerted effort to make the public asylum system humane, providing places of healing for pauper patients who had nowhere else to go.

A number of factors may have contributed to the development of this new system in England. Understanding of mental illness as *illness* rather than *badness* or *madness* may have been hastened by King George III, who suffered from periodic psychosis throughout his reign and died insane in 1820. The most important factor, however, was probably the change in social conditions brought about by the industrial revolution, which created a crowded and overworked urban working-class population. Where ill family members might formerly have been sheltered on the family farm, the new transient reality and stresses of city living left few supports for the mentally fragile.

In 1845, the English Parliament passed a bill that required all counties to set up public asylums for paupers. This public system would be overseen by the Lunacy Commission, which would ensure asylums offered consistent and ethical medical care. Instead of being detained in jails and workhouses,

mentally ill patients would be provided with shelter and treatment. Earlier in the century, a movement in England to abolish restraints had taken hold, and by 1850, physical restraints had been eliminated from public asylums.

Asylums endeavoured to provide a healthy environment; good food; occupation in the gardens, workshops, and laundries; and entertainment such as dances, plays, choirs, and magic-lantern shows. Medication and other forms of physical treatment, such as shower baths, sedatives, exercise, and purgatives, were prescribed as required. The average stay in the Surrey asylum at this time was four and a half years. Unfortunately, the optimistic view that severe mental illness could be consistently treated was to last only a few decades. By the 1880s, the overcrowding in public asylums resulted in the reintroduction of the physical—and eventually "chemical"—restraints still evident in psychiatric hospitals today.

Although these photographs are unsettling, it is reassuring to know that the women in these first medical photographs probably received good care. These photographs give me this hope. The individuality evident in each not only reveals the photographer's skill, but also acknowledges each woman's unique experience of being human.

Cinéma Vérité

BRAD CRAN

Cinéma-vérité means that we have wanted to eliminate fiction and get closer to real life. We know that we must only pose the problem of truth.

— Jean Rouch

Ravished Armenia

Aurora Mardiganian was sixteen in 1917 when she fled the genocide in Armenia via Russia and sailed from Oslo to the United States in search of her one surviving brother. Among other atrocities, she had witnessed Turkish soldiers slice her aunt open, pull a baby from her womb, and pound it to pulp with the butt of a rifle. Aurora arrived at Ellis Island and was taken in by an Armenian couple who promptly placed advertisements in newspapers in an attempt to locate her brother. She was discovered by the New York media, and soon afterwards, she became the ward of Harvey Gates, a screenwriter who arranged for the translation of Aurora's story into the best-selling book *Ravished Armenia*. Gates then sold the screenplay for thousands of dollars and had Aurora sign a contract to play the lead for fifteen dollars a week.

In Los Angeles on the first day of shooting, when actors walked onto the set wearing Turkish fezzes, Aurora assumed that she had been tricked and would be executed. In filming her escape from a fabricated Turkish harem, the filmmakers had Aurora jump between two rooftops, but she fell twenty feet, broke her ankle, and had to be carried from scene to scene for the rest of the production.

Under the auspices of the American Committee for Armenian and Syrian Relief, the film was released with press packages that read "*Ravished Armenia* to show real harems" and "With other naked girls, pretty Aurora Mardiganian was sold for eighty-five cents."

Gates and his wife were then paid seven thousand dollars to ensure that Aurora appeared at screenings of the film. Aurora received none of this money, which she desperately needed to bring her sister to the United States. Aurora detested the promotional dinner parties and fundraisers, and she openly stated her desire to be alone. She was deemed incapable of dealing with the promotion on the film and sent to a convent school, while seven Aurora impersonators promoted the film, which had been renamed *Auction of Souls*.

Combat America

Hitler invaded Poland, the Japanese attacked Pearl Harbor, and dreams of American isolation died, but the world did not stop for Clark Gable. He and his wife, Carole Lombard, offered their services to the White House and were told to continue making patriotic movies. While on tour selling war bonds, Lombard was killed in a plane crash near Las Vegas. President Franklin D. Roosevelt decorated Lombard posthumously and offered a military funeral, but Gable refused the honour and buried his wife in a small ceremony in Glendale, California.

General Henry H. Arnold, commander of the Army Air Corps, needed gunners for flying fortresses, so he approached Gable about enlisting for the position to boost recruitment and make a documentary about his experience. *Combat America* was released in 1943. MGM publicists tried to persuade the army to recruit Gable as a captain, consistent with the roles he played on screen, but Arnold insisted that the actor enlist at the bottom and earn his rank through the Officer Candidate School.

The army roped off half a floor of the Los Angeles Federal Building to swear in Gable and his friend, cinematographer Andrew McIntyre. Afterwards, Gable told the press that he had enlisted as a gunner, and the MGM publicity department released his serial number so fans could memorize it.

While Gable served guard duty, women from the adjacent town stood on the outside of the fence and peppered him with crumpled balls of paper bearing their phone numbers. Around his neck, Gable kept a small gold box that held pieces of his dead wife's jewellery, and when he refused to leave his post one night during a lightning storm, rumours spread that he wanted to join her in the grave.

After he finished his training, Gable received his uniform, which he sent to the MGM costume department to be altered, so that it better fit his physique. Gable arrived in Britain with the 351st Bomb Group, led by Lieutenant Colonel William A. Hatcher, and they were greeted on Nazi broadcast radio by the British traitor Lord Haw-Haw. "Welcome to England, Hatcher's Chickens, among whom is the famous American cinema star, Clark Gable. We'll be seeing you soon in Germany, Clark."

Hitler admired Gable and hoped he would be captured alive and brought to him in Berlin. Gable had changed his name from the German "Goebel," which the Nazis embraced as proof that he was closely related to their minister of propaganda, Joseph Goebbels. Gable was therefore a trophy for both sides. Hermann Göring offered a cash reward to any Luftwaffe pilot who shot down the plane carrying the star of *Gone with the Wind*.

Kolberg

Hitler wept as Joseph Goebbels described scenes from the film *Kolberg*, in which the cast re-enacts the successful defence of a small German town against Napoleon's army in 1807. In the sixth year of World War II, both Hitler and Goebbels knew that they must reinvigorate the flagging spirits of the German people, and they felt that screenings of *Kolberg* (1945) would boost morale as much as a real military victory on the battlefields that were closing in around them. The film begins with a note incorrectly stating that production of the film started in 1942, so that the German people would not think that the film was made in response to the catastrophe of Stalingrad or the Luftwaffe's growing inability to defend German cities against Allied bombs.

Goebbels revised the major patriotic speeches in the film and instructed Veit Harlan, the director, to work a love interest into the story. After viewing rough cuts, Goebbels ordered Harlan to make the film more like the Academy Award–winning work *Mrs. Miniver*, about an English woman's resolve during the German bombing of London.

Kolberg premiered in the besieged fortress of La Rochelle in occupied France, after it was parachuted in to be played for the Nazi soldiers who had been ordered to keep the city at all costs.

In 1945, the city of Kolberg again came under attack. When the commandant in charge proposed to Hitler that the city be surrendered, he was dismissed and replaced by a younger officer, who fought until Kolberg fell a few days later, after severe casualties were inflicted. Goebbels refused to acknowledge the fall of Kolberg, and he squelched all news of the loss in his military report, because he did not want the loss of the town to affect the power of the movie.

The Short and Once Happy Life of Kurt Gerron

As an actor in German silent films and a regular cabaret performer, Kurt Gerron was a darling of Berlin, but he did not become a star until 1928, when he performed in his friend Bertolt Brecht's play *The Threepenny Opera* and became the first person to sing "Mack the Knife." Gerron also acted alongside Marlene Dietrich in Josef von Sternberg's *The Blue Angel* before Dietrich defected to the United States. Hitler's rise to power seemed comic to Gerron right up until the day all Jews were ordered out of the entertainment industry in Germany and the actor was forced to leave his belongings and his home for Paris, where he begged for work.

Gerron's friend Peter Lorre, who had suffered a similar fate, withered in Paris. Penniless and sick,

Lorre decided to try his luck in Hollywood. To help him, Gerron took up a collection among the German acting community. Gerron found work directing and soon received word from Hollywood that Lorre had become, in the words of Charlie Chaplin, the world's greatest actor. To thank his friend, Lorre arranged for Warner Brothers to ship Gerron to Hollywood. But Gerron requested first-class passage, and when this was denied, he took work directing a film in Amsterdam, where he became active in the Dutch Municipal Theatre and a local Jewish theatre.

Shortly after the Nazis marched into Holland, Gerron arrived at work to find that the municipal theatre had been transformed into a deportation centre for the transfer of Jews to Auschwitz. The Nazis appointed Gerron to take charge of people deemed lost or found.

After his duties were completed, Gerron was herded into a cattle car bound for Theresienstadt, a concentration camp that received many high-profile Jews whom the Nazis wanted to keep at the ready in case neutral European countries charged that all Jews were being sent to their deaths.

The inmates of the Theresienstadt ghetto were kept barely alive. Gerron lost much of the weight that had made his face famous in Berlin. He acted each night in a ghetto cabaret. One afternoon, as the actors arrived to prepare for the evening performance, they found that their makeshift theatre had been filled to the ceiling with the corpses of fellow Jews. They emptied the theatre by passing the bodies down a line, and that night, they performed as usual.

Under pressure to convince neutral European countries that the Jews were being treated properly, the Nazis agreed to allow the Red Cross to visit Theresienstadt. Transportations to the east stopped, the entire camp was cleaned, and the Jews of Theresienstadt were required to participate in a variety of cultural activities. The commandant requested that Gerron make a film about the high quality of life in Theresienstadt. Fifteen Jews had already been executed for creating drawings that accurately depicted life in the concentration camp, so Gerron sought advice from the council of elders, who told him to do whatever it took to stay alive.

Gerron began work on his final film, *The Führer Gives a City to the Jews*. Gerron filmed symphonies, soccer games, and children eating bread. He filmed boys and girls swimming in the newly built swimming pool and singing in the choir. "As a director," Gerron said, "I can direct the scene, but I cannot remove the horror from their eyes."

The Red Cross deemed Theresienstadt to provide many luxuries that were scarce even in Prague. When Gerron finished filming, transportations resumed, and almost all the men, women, and children who had appeared in his film were shipped to Auschwitz.

Despite the blessing of the council of elders, Gerron was ostracized for working so diligently on the film. Still, he thought that his life might be spared. But the transportations continued, and he was transported east on the last cattle car out of Theresienstadt to Auschwitz. There, on the last day that the fires burned, he was placed in an oven and incinerated.

Marlene Dietrich

After starring as the seductress Lola Lola in Josef von Sternberg's 1930 hit *The Blue Angel*, Marlene Dietrich signed a contract with Paramount and left Berlin for Hollywood. Paramount promoted her as an undiscovered star rather than a veteran German actress who had already performed in more than a dozen films. She became a star in America after the release of *Morocco* (1930), in which she appeared opposite Gary Cooper, wore pants, and kissed a woman.

However, after *Morocco*, Dietrich made half-a-dozen poorly received Hollywood films and was deemed box-office poison. Theatre owners wrote to the studios, asking them not to cast her, and producer David O. Selznick said that despite Dietrich's original fame, no personality could survive the lineup of dreadful pictures that she had made.

Adolf Hitler and Joseph Goebbels disagreed. They wanted Dietrich to denounce the Jews of Hollywood and return to Germany to become the Queen of Third Reich cinema. Joachim von Ribbentrop, Hitler's foreign minister, personally visited Dietrich to offer her stardom in Germany, but the actress took American citizenship instead and was declared an enemy who had abandoned the fatherland for Jews.

In Hollywood, Dietrich housed expatriate artists who had fled Europe to escape the Nazis. She fell in love with Jean Gabin, an actor who had joined the French Resistance as a tank commander. Dietrich enlisted in the army to entertain Allied troops and to sell war bonds to buy bombs to drop on Berlin, the city where her mother, Josephine, continued to live.

Dietrich performed on stage and, afterwards, insisted on being taken to the front, where she sang and flirted with the soldiers to briefly take their minds off the war. During the Battle of the Bulge, she came within a hundred yards of being captured by Nazi soldiers. While away from the front, she recorded German folk songs for the Office of Strategic Services (later renamed the Central Intelligence Agency), and these songs were broadcast on the front lines to make Nazi soldiers homesick. Dwight D. Eisenhower declared that no man, woman, actor, or film star had done more for the morale of the Allied troops than Marlene Dietrich, and in 1947, she became the first woman to be awarded the Medal of Freedom.

When Allied forces moved into Germany, she followed the troops in, entertaining them in a bombed-out theatre in Aachen. As the Allies pushed east and learned of the mass extermination of Jews, Dietrich flew to Bergen-Belsen, where she learned that her sister's husband had worked as a special services officer in charge of the canteen and movie theatre that entertained the Nazi soldiers who worked in the concentration camp. Of the forty thousand Jews rescued from Bergen-Belsen, twenty-eight thousand died of starvation and typhus within days of their liberation. Dietrich was among the first Americans to visit the camp and see the thousands of corpses overflowing the mass graves.

Her sister, who had also worked at the Nazi theatre, told Dietrich that their mother had survived and was living in Berlin, though her apartment had been destroyed by Allied bombs. Dietrich left Bergen-Belsen and never again publicly acknowledged the existence of her sister. An American soldier was assigned to search the rubble of Berlin for Josephine Dietrich, and she was found living in a small room—in poverty, but happy that she had outlived "that bastard" Hitler. Josephine was taken to a field phone and patched through to Marlene, who cried and said, "Mama, Mama, forgive me."

The Pint-Sized Gary Cooper

Weighing in at 110 pounds, Audie Murphy had already been turned down for service in the Marines and the Paratroopers in 1942 when an army recruitment officer reluctantly accepted his application to join the infantry. At boot camp, Murphy's sergeant nicknamed him "Baby" and tried to have him transferred to the cooks and bakers' school. Murphy refused the transfer and completed his basic training in the smallest combat boots the army had, but they were still three sizes too big for his feet.

When Murphy arrived on the shores of Sicily, his commander tried to keep him out of combat by making him a runner, but at every opportunity, Murphy sneaked off on patrols in hopes of reaching the front. Eventually, his commander relented, and Murphy saw his first action on the northern coast of the island, where he earned a reputation as a quick thinker who was able to attack when the enemy expected a retreat.

When in France he faced a barrage of German tanks and soldiers, Murphy called the men in his platoon back while he stayed in position to call in artillery strikes on the advancing Germans. The dispatcher asked how close the enemy was and Murphy replied, "If you'll just hold the phone, I'll let you talk to one of the bastards."

When the Germans were mere yards away, Murphy jumped atop a burning, bombed-out tank destroyer, removed the dead body that sat in front of the mounted 50-calibre gun, and began firing. As they approached the tank destroyer, he called in an artillery attack on his own position. The Germans pulled back, and Murphy hopped off the tank destroyer moments before it exploded. He was not injured by the Germans or his own artillery, but he bled profusely from a recent shrapnel injury that should have kept him in the hospital that day.

For his bravery, Murphy was awarded the Congressional Medal of Honor, but he refused to travel to Washington for a presidential ceremony and was instead awarded the medal in the field, so he could continue to fight with his company. By the end of his military career, Murphy had spent four hundred days on the front lines and had become the most decorated combat soldier to fight in World War II, credited with killing or capturing 240 Germans.

Murphy returned to a hero's welcome in San Antonio, Texas. Shortly afterwards, acting veteran James Cagney—who had transformed himself from a Yorkville drag queen into a wisecracking war hero—offered Murphy an all-expenses-paid trip to Hollywood.

Shortly after his twenty-first birthday in 1945, Audie Murphy signed a $150-a-week contract with James Cagney, on the condition that he enrol in the Actor's Laboratory to study singing, dancing, and swordsmanship. He landed an eight-word part in *Beyond Glory* but admitted that the role required seven more words than he could handle. For the next two years, he struggled to find work. When his contract with Cagney expired, Murphy moved into a Beverly Hills gymnasium owned by a patriotic admirer.

David McClure, assistant to the gossip columnist Hedda Hopper, was disgusted that America's greatest war hero was living in a gymnasium. Using Hopper's influence, McClure helped Murphy land a few more Hollywood roles. Eventually, the aspiring actor landed the part of Billy the Kid in *The Kid from Texas*, which launched his twenty-year career in B-movie westerns.

In *The Red Badge of Courage*, Murphy was cast opposite Bill Mauldin, who had been stationed in Italy during the war as a cartoonist for *Stars and Stripes*. In a scene where Murphy was to confess to Mauldin that he ran from battle, Murphy broke down on set and said, "I can't confess a thing like that to this rear-echelon ink slinger." The script was then changed to have Mauldin confess his cowardice to Murphy, and shooting resumed.

On set, Murphy ate lunch with the extras and stuntmen. He detested Hollywood stars and kept to himself, except during his first days in the city, when actors lined up to shake his hand. His first Hollywood love left him for Howard Hughes, and the actress he married divorced him on the grounds of emotional cruelty. One morning, when he and his second wife were on their honeymoon, she woke to find him sitting up in bed holding the loaded German pistol that he slept with every night. Murphy suffered from a seven-year bout of insomnia. He became addicted to the tranquilizers and eventually moved his bedroom into his garage, where he felt he could better defend himself.

When Murphy's stature as a war hero began to fade from public memory, McClure ghostwrote the actor's autobiography, which the publisher titled *To Hell and Back*. Most of the details of Murphy's life were too traumatic for him to talk about, so McClure filled in the gaps with the citations from Murphy's twenty-seven military medals.

Universal optioned *To Hell and Back* with plans to cast Tony Curtis as Murphy, but Murphy disliked Curtis and fancied playing the role himself.

Seeing *To Hell and Back* as "a vitamin pill for recruiting," army officials put an entire division at the disposal of the studio and agreed to back the film with a million dollars in men and equipment. Then they created the Audie Murphy Platoon, whose first fifty members would be recruited by Murphy at the movie's San Antonio premiere in 1955.

During the shooting of *To Hell and Back*, the army held a full-scale divisional review in Murphy's honour. For an hour and a half, twenty thousand men, including artillery, trucks, and jeeps, marched past Murphy, who refused to take a seat and remained standing until every man had gone by. Afterwards he said, "I think I'll re-enlist."

Breaking the Blacklist

When the American Legion learned that Dalton Trumbo had been hired to write the screenplay for Stanley Kubrick's *Spartacus* (1960), the military veterans' organization sent out seventeen thousand letters to their posts, encouraging members to picket the film and uphold the blacklist that had been championed by Ronald Reagan. But the movie's star, Kirk Douglas—who had insisted that Trumbo receive credit for his work—was larger than anti-Communist paranoia, and moviegoers lined up for blocks to see the film despite American Legion pickets. Earlier, *Spartacus* had been censored by the Production Code Administration, not because of any Communist ideals that Trumbo had slipped into the film, but because of the suggestion that Crassus felt homosexual desire for the slave Antonius. In the scene in question, Crassus asks Antonius if he eats oysters or snails or, as Crassus prefers, oysters and snails. The Catholic Legion of Decency also ordered that violence be cut from the film and that the film be scrutinized to ensure that the loincloths covered the actors' genitals. Shortly after the release of the film, the picket lines dispersed, and *Spartacus* later won four Academy Awards. Ronald Reagan did not publicly state his disapproval of either the Communist screenwriter or the homosexual innuendo, but later, as governor of California, he affirmed his aversion to Communists, and when asked if homosexuals should be barred from public office, he said that they should certainly be barred from the Department of Beaches and Parks.

Best Supporting Role

In April 1978, outside the Dorothy Chandler Pavilion where the 50th Academy Awards ceremony was to be held, the Jewish Defense League burned Vanessa Redgrave in effigy while chanting "Arafat's whore!" A few feet away, a group of American Arabs gathered and waved the Palestinian flag. While making the film *Julia*, for which she was nominated for the best-supporting-actress award, Redgrave had roomed with students who were in exile from occupied Palestine. Their stories of oppression under Zionism drove Redgrave to sell her house to fund the documentary *The Palestinian*, which eventually included a conversation she had with Yasser Arafat. During the publicity tour for *Julia*, Redgrave held private screenings of *The Palestinian* for filmmakers and public broadcasting producers, who would not consider showing the film for fear of losing their oil-company sponsorships. When a

theatre in Los Angeles agreed to screen the film, its box office was bombed by the Jewish Defense League, whose members told Twentieth Century Fox that they would cause every kind of problem unless Fox issued a statement saying that it would never hire Redgrave again. The press dubbed Redgrave a terrorist, and *The Palestinian* was banned in Israel.

Redgrave did indeed win the Oscar that night for her portrayal of Julia, a freedom fighter who lost her life trying to smuggle Jews out of Nazi Germany. In her acceptance speech, Redgrave thanked the Academy for not bowing to the pressure of "Zionist hoodlums" and reiterated her commitment to fight anti-Semitism and fascism. She did this, although Howard W. Koch, chairman of the Academy Awards Committee, had warned her that snipers would be present for her own security and urged her, if she won, simply to say "Thank you."

Schindler's List

On Martin Luther King Day in 1994, a group of students, most of them black, was ejected from the Grand Lake Theater in Oakland, California, after ten of them laughed during an execution scene in Steven Spielberg's movie *Schindler's List*. The students filed out of the theatre to the cheers and applause of the other patrons—some of whom had survived the very Holocaust that Spielberg was portraying. Four months later, Spielberg and California governor Pete Wilson visited the ejected students' Oakland high school to talk to the teenagers and to promote The Schindler's List Project, which would allow sixteen thousand students a week the opportunity to view *Schindler's List* free of charge. The project would also supply each student with a pamphlet that provided information about anti-Semitism and the events of the Holocaust and urged students to respect the serious nature of the violence in the film by abstaining from eating popcorn and drinking soda pop.

On their arrival at the high school, Spielberg and Wilson were met by 250 members of the media and 150 protesters who carried signs with messages such as "Spielberg, don't teach us about racism, oppression and genocide." Inside the auditorium where Spielberg spoke, students were vocal about wanting to learn more about Martin Luther King and the history of their own people before learning about the oppression of white people.

In Malaysia, censors banned *Schindler's List* as Jewish propaganda that "reflects the privilege and virtues of a certain race only." The Committee for World Muslim Solidarity denounced the film as Zionist propaganda, and it was later banned in Syria, Lebanon, Jordan, and Egypt. In the Philippines, censors objected to a scene in which Oskar Schindler makes love to his mistress with the distinct pumping motion of sexual intercourse. "If a person is poor," the censor stated, "and he gets horny, he's just going to rape." He therefore suggested that people who wanted to view *Schindler's List* should do so on video so that they could have their "private orgasm" in the privacy of their room.

Kundun

Among his godly acts as a politician, Henry Kissinger brought fire and napalm to the people of Vietnam in the name of fighting Communism in Asia. He began his service in the Nixon administration not after Richard Nixon's inauguration but days before the 1968 election, when he visited Paris as an illegal American envoy charged with the task of persuading the South Vietnamese to reject Lyndon Johnson's plan to end the war in Vietnam.

Kissinger succeeded in dissuading the South Vietnamese from accepting the peace plan of the Democratic president. Nixon was elected, and the war in Vietnam raged for another four years, resulting in the deaths of incalculable Vietnamese people and of at least twenty thousand American soldiers.

Later, the Nixon administration ended the war in Vietnam with a proposal that was identical to the Democratic proposal that Kissinger had quashed in Paris four years earlier. Kissinger then arranged

Nixon's historic handshake with Mao Zedong, which led to the United States' official recognition of Communist China. For his efforts in encouraging the recognition of China in the West, Kissinger commands great respect and is referred to as an "old friend" of the people. He also earned admiration for his public and political defence of the Chinese government's slaughter of its children in Tiananmen Square.

While giving out the Oscar for best art direction at the 1993 Academy Awards, Richard Gere asked the audience to mentally send love and truth and sanity to Deng Xiaoping so that he would pull his troops from Tibet and allow Tibetans to live as free and independent people. Gere later made the film *Red Corner*, in which the protagonist is caught up in the ruthless grasp of the heartless government of China.

Disney produced *Kundun*, which favourably portrayed the life of the Dalai Lama and, therefore, unfavourably portrayed the repressive Chinese government, which was angered not only because of the subject matter, but also because the Dalai Lama's niece played a part in the film and because the scriptwriter, Melissa Mathison, and her husband, Harrison Ford, had spent six days with the Dalai Lama in Dharmsala, India. There, Ford had read the script to the Dalai Lama while Mathison took notes on his holiness's various reactions. The Chinese government warned Disney that it would suffer severe economic reprisal if the film was released.

Rather than shelving the $28-million production, Disney released *Kundun* on Christmas Day 1997 and hired Henry Kissinger as an envoy to help Disney expand its $24-billion industry into the massive Chinese market. Kissinger had already broken down barriers in China for Heinz, Coca-Cola, and Revlon and was sure to open the market for Mickey Mouse toys and *Pocahontas* videos, despite Martin Scorsese's *Kundun*, which in Tibetan means "the presence of a great incarnation."

Making Black Hawk Down

Despite the objections of senior White House staff members, Secretary of Defense Donald Rumsfeld approved the dispatching of eight helicopters and one hundred soldiers to Morocco in 2001, creating the first American military operation orchestrated on foreign soil solely for the purpose of shooting a Hollywood movie. The film was to be a gritty and realistic depiction of the 1993 Battle of Mogadishu, in which eighteen American soldiers lost their lives and some of the bloated corpses were dragged through the streets of the Somalian capital.

Rumsfeld vetted the script and demanded specific changes. The helicopters and soldiers were deployed shortly after filming began. Director Ridley Scott and producer Jerry Bruckheimer had agreed to modify the script in order to secure the Black Hawks and the soldiers who occupied the set in plain clothes while actors in army fatigues re-enacted the fierce battle. Cast members, most of them British, had gone through a somewhat rigorous boot camp in the United States so that they could properly represent the American soldiers who had fought and been killed in the battle.

The changes requested by Rumsfeld and the Pentagon were not made public, but the final script omitted the efforts of United Nations soldiers, particularly the Malaysians, who had rescued the stranded American soldiers. Instead, the film suggested that the inaction of the United Nations forces had caused many of the American casualties.

During test screenings, the film contained a postscript that said the events of Somalia depicted in the film had inspired and set the mentality for the September 11, 2001, attacks on the United States. Test audiences found the postscript offensive. The release date was then moved up at the request of the Pentagon, which had recently put Somalia at the top of its list of countries ripe for American invasion.

The producers held the world premiere of *Black Hawk Down* in Washington. Shortly afterwards, a bootleg copy was smuggled into Mogadishu and premiered just a mile from the original battle site, where the eighteen Americans and more than a thousand Somalis were killed. At the Mogadishu premiere, Somalis paid about ten cents each to watch the film. As American soldiers died on screen, the Somalis cheered and celebrated. CNN aired exclusive footage of this small screening and the audience's reaction. The American media reported heavily on the pleasure that Somalis took in seeing American soldiers killed and juxtaposed these reports with the images of a small group of Somalis dragging American soldiers through the streets of Mogadishu on the day when more than a thousand of their people had been killed by Americans.

Rumsfeld was keen to invade Somalia, but instead, he set his sights higher and helped the Bush administration overcome the will of the United Nations in order to invade Iraq. In the White House, George W. Bush screened *Black Hawk Down* and declared it his favourite film.

In Malaysia, there was a movement to ban the film because of its historical inaccuracies and its failure to acknowledge the Malay soldiers who had risked their lives to save the Americans. One of these men had died, and others had received letters from the American soldiers thanking them for their lives.

Other high-ranking Malays said that the movie should be viewed as entertainment in the same manner as a Sylvester Stallone *Rocky* film. The Malaysian controversy was then overshadowed by international speculation that the United States would invade Somalia once it was finished in Afghanistan, because popular support to return to Mogadishu was on the rise in the U.S.A.

Black Hawk Down *Memorial*

As America prepared to invade Iraq, Saddam Hussein circulated copies of *Black Hawk Down* (2001) to his troops and insisted that they watch it as an instruction manual for killing American soldiers. In the film, as in the real Battle of Mogadishu, eighteen American soldiers were killed. In the first year of the invasion and subsequent occupation of Iraq, Iraqi insurgents killed more than five hundred American soldiers and shot down more than ten helicopters. Mark Bowden, who wrote *Black Hawk Down*, bought a Corvette and built "The Black Hawk Down Memorial Swimming Pool" in his backyard. After a day on the movie set in Morocco, an army helicopter pilot offered Bowden a ride tethered to the outside bench of an

MH6 Little Bird, in the same manner as the original U.S. Army Rangers had been transported into Mogadishu. The helicopter lifted Bowden above the effigies of downed Black Hawks and over the mosques of Morocco so that he could see the sunset over the Atlantic Ocean. He described the experience as a magic carpet ride and said that he was thinking all the while, What a lucky son of a bitch I am.

Hollywood and the Fate of the Hero

After earning the Bronze Star for "extreme courage" in the Battle of Mogadishu, Aaron Weaver was stricken with testicular cancer and was bedridden while enduring treatment for the disease. The cancer went into remission and Weaver, despite having lost a significant amount of weight, persuaded army physicians to allow him to deploy to Iraq in 2003 to fly helicopter missions alongside his brothers Steve and Ryan in the war against terrorism.

The army arranged for Weaver to have his cancer checkups in a medical centre in Baghdad, and he was flying there in a Black Hawk when it was hit by an insurgent's rocket and plummeted into a potato field outside the city of Fallujah. The crash killed Weaver and eight other soldiers, but it was Weaver and the Black Hawk that most interested the media. Nine men had died, but only Weaver had first survived the battle that became the movie *Black Hawk Down*, only to go on to beat cancer and insist on serving his country despite his health.

He was a hero who made it to the end of the film.

Weaver's father said it was hard to believe that his son had survived the Battle of Mogadishu and testicular cancer, only to be shot down in a Black Hawk that was not even engaged in combat and bore the sign of the Red Cross. His father then pleaded with the army to remove his two other sons from the combat zones, as was done for the fictional last surviving son of Mrs. Margaret Ryan in *Saving Private Ryan*.

Weaver had often talked about the Battle of Mogadishu and said that the film *Black Hawk Down* had helped him come to terms with the fact that he was put in a position where he had to kill people needlessly. Two days before his death, he had phoned his father and asked for books rather than food because mice were getting to the food before he was. His father had planned to send him a couple of novels and books on astrology.

Washington Square Park in the afternoon... (cherryblossoms)

Pages from a Sketchbook

CHRIS WARE

The clean lines of Chris Ware's work may appear deceptively simple to the inexperienced reader. But behind the cartoonist's hand lurks a novelist's mind. Fans who purchased The Acme Novelty Datebook *(Drawn and Quarterly Books, 2003) were given a chance to see beyond the cartoons into the diverse visual imagination of a true craftsman. This collection of sketches, still lifes, cartoons, and ponderings presented a rich narrative of the artist's scope and creative genius. Ware's work passes through the influences of Gustav Doré, Charles Schultz, Robert Crumb, and Hergé, to arrive at a style that is inimitable. In the following pages,* Brick *is very proud to present a selection from the forthcoming second volume of the* Datebooks.

OUT "L'ECLAIREUR'S" FRONT DOOR 8/1.

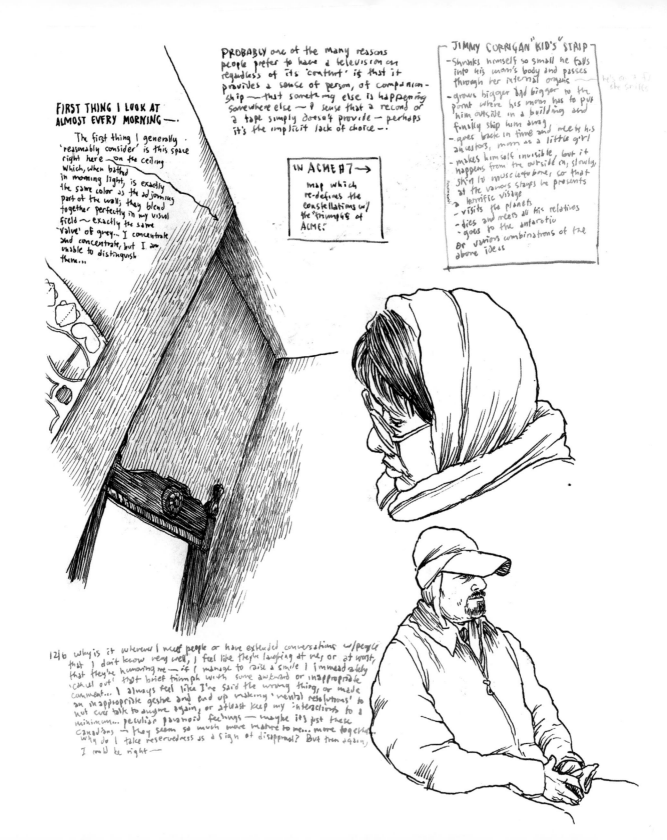

FIRST THING I LOOK AT ALMOST EVERY MORNING —.

The first thing I generally 'reasonably consider' is this space right here — on the ceiling which, when bathed in morning light, is exactly the same color as the adjoining part of the wall; they blend together perfectly in my visual field — exactly the same 'value' of grey... I concentrate and concentrate, but I am unable to distinguish them...

PROBABLY one of the many reasons people prefer to have a television on regardless of its 'content' is that it provides a sense of person, of companionship — that something else is happening somewhere else — a sense that a record or a tape simply doesn't provide — perhaps it's the implicit lack of choice —.

IN ACME #7 →
map which re-defines the constellations w/ the "triumph of ACME."

JIMMY CORRIGAN "KID'S" STRIP —
- Shrinks himself so small he falls into his mom's body and passes through her internal organs —
- grows bigger and bigger to the point where his mom has to put him outside in a building and finally ship him away
- goes back in time and meets his ancestors, mom as a little girl
- makes himself invisible, but it happens from the outside in, slowly, skin to muscle to bone, so that at the various stages he presents a horrific visage
- visits the planets
- visits all his relatives
- dies and meets all his relatives
- goes to the antarctic
or various combinations of the above ideas

12/6 why is it whenever I meet people or have extended conversations w/ people that I don't know very well, I feel like they're laughing at me or at worst, that they're humoring me — if I manage to raise a smile I immediately 'cancel out' that brief triumph with some awkward or inappropriate comment... I always feel like I've said the wrong thing, or made an inappropriate gesture and end up making 'mental resolutions' to not ever talk to anyone again, or at least keep my interactions to a minimum... peculiar paranoid feelings — maybe it's just these Canadians — they seem so much more mature to me... more together... why do I take reservedness as a sign of disapproval? But then again I could be right —

HOPELESS

people keep coming in and visiting me...
I am having many visitors... but they
never say anything, they simply stop and
stare, like they're wearing masks...

My legs feel heavy sometimes

FLIGHT BACK from AMSTERDAM 1/17.

SPIEGELMAN LIVING ROOM 7/4.
evening light—

shelf w/toys & knick knacks.

anything to say to him, I was so hyper-conscious of the
feeling that he disliked me...peculiar— most of them talked
to make each other laugh, like friends do... but it was hard
for me to enter a situation like that— Maybe they all think I'm
just an arrogant little cocky idiot or something... I know I
was extra boring... couldn't think of anything to say... rarely
met people's gaze...I felt like a real idiot. Times like these I
think I should just not ever meet anyone...

SPIEGELMAN FAMILY BEDROOM 7/4. afternoon light

IRRITATING
"ONE MAN BAND"
AT RESTAURANT
IN ST. GEORGES ~ 8/1.

ACME # 8 — Old Chicago ~ funeral, etc ~ World's Fair.
ACME # 9 — Doctor's Office
ACME #10 — Catalogue/ J.C. Story
ACME # 11 — Old Chicago
ACME # 12 — Restaurant.

— Jimmy & his Dad happen upon one of his Dad's "friends" who gives them a ride back to the apartment — friendly conversation ensues, regarding "Amy", Dad, work, etc. Jimmy falls into a bit of a daze, looking out the window at passing details, and the backs of the two men's heads...

— Back home, his Dad "sets him up" in the bedroom for a 'rest' and Jimmy finds a photo album w/ pictures of his Dad's second marriage... and his adoptive daughter...

BE AS IGNORANT AS POSSIBLE of
ALL CONTEMPORARY CLICHÉS and
"DEVICES" of PACING!!

IN ACME #8:
"Money" to cut out & spend.

These are
actually all
pine trees

though they
don't look
like them

people &
servants
everywhere...

(DAD & MOM'S HOUSE)

LAKE HOUSE WHERE
PHIL & SUE GOT MARRIED. 8/3.

from *The Japan Journals*

DONALD RICHIE

1 June 1995. Susan [Sontag], Annie [Leibowitz], Ian [Buruma], and I went to the opening of the Araki [Nobuyoshi] photo show. Four walls of naked girls sporting their pubic hair while being tied up, strapped down, and otherwise held into place—a display little differing (except in size) from what is found in the pages of s/m albums. That, and the fact that it was public. It would not have been allowed five years ago.

This I tell Susan. "Progress?" she asks rhetorically, then, "How any woman could look at this and not feel angry I just don't know." Ian says, "Well, you know, it is really ritual display, nothing moral about it, just narcissistic." "Just!" says Susan. "Nothing moral!" says Susan. And Annie says, "Well, it makes me feel hungry."

Agreed, we go to Shin Okubo, and before eating at the Shin Sekai, I take them on a tour of the Hyakunincho. But also taking tours are lots of cop cars, and they drive the girls off the street. I talk to one fleeing group. "Are the cops dangerous?" I ask. "Not really," says one— South American perhaps, in good Japanese—"but a royal pain in the ass (*mattaku mendokusai*)."

At the restaurant we eat fish and frog. Annie tells about when she was first in Japan, as a child, taken on the crowded subway: "And when we got off, my dress was up to here!"— points to her ribs, indicating, I think, the press of the crowds. Susan says that when she comes to Japan she feels like a European going to America. The new world, the twenty-first century, the burgeoning of the coming.

30 April 2002. Out with Susan—had not seen her since last fall when she came to my Japan Society dinner right after she had been attacked on TV for writing her courageous assessment of the World Trade Center attack. In the short *New Yorker* piece she reminded the U.S.A. that there were reasons for its being so hated—that is all. "Oh, it got worse," she says in that fine way she has, as though speaking of someone else. "Death threats, midnight calls." I say that if that happened to me I would have folded up. "No you wouldn't, you just think you would. Anyway, you just wait till they stop." I ask what kind of people. "Oh, professional people, intellectuals, no low-life." She tells me that *The New Republic* had an article that began by rhetorically asking: What do Saddam Hussein, Osama bin Laden, and Susan Sontag have in common? Then answering with: They all wish the destruction of America.

Susan Sontag and Donald Richie

It is holiday season, Golden Week, and she remarks that there are no Japanese flags. We compare this with the U.S.A., where the American flag is now the most commonly found decoration—Stars and Stripes just everywhere, a country swathed in bunting. We discuss the implications of this triumphalism. "Well," she says, "this is the first time in history that one country has had this much power."

3 May 2002. Susan and I go to Asakusa, where we went during her first trip, more than a decade ago. "How clean it all is," she says. "I remember it being much more scruffy." Asakusa has been gentrified, turned into taxidermy, I say. We tour the neat little clutch of Edo temples, and she notices that they all now look plastic, even the real ones.

What will happen to Japan, she wonders, and guesses that the first thing to really go will be the banks. I tell her that everyone is now living on his or her fat, and since Japan was financially obese there is a lot of that. She tells me a "joke" that her son, David, told her: What is the difference between Japan and Argentina? Answer: Three years.

She finds much else different and at the same time now sees things she formerly did not. "These people do not know how to have discourse." Invited here for one of these expensive "conferences" among intellectuals, she tells me what it is like, and gives a very funny impersonation of a famous Japanese architect making a presentation. "And I saw this building. And it was very big. And I thought, This is big, very big."

I mention that the language does not really accommodate discourse, but it does encourage analogical talk, one thing leading to another, and I mention that in Japan it is *suji* instead of plot. At once Susan is interested. With her it is a way of learning.

Out comes the notebook and *suji* is spelled out. I tell her about favoured form, which looks no better written than it seems spoken: "following the brush" (*zuihitsu*), spontaneous nattering. I suggest that this is what the other people in the conference were up to. She writes all this down, and at once agrees that there are, certainly, different modes of thought, then she stops.

"Still, everyone is so corrupt—intellectually, morally." We cast about for reasons why this should be so, and she, only here a couple of times, hits upon the one real answer: "It is because everyone is afraid. They do not want to be punished. And this country is so crony-prone, so given to authority, that if you do speak out, if you are intellectually honest, you will certainly be punished. If the people on my panel spoke out they would not get invited to the next panel, architects would not get commissions. That is what I mean by corrupt."

Corrupt Susan is certainly not. Have I ever known anyone more honest, more forthright, more brave? I think not—nor anyone more moral. She can cut through cant, can see through any amount of bad faith. Just to be with her is to think more clearly, to become more courageous.

16 October 2002. Most of my life has been spent regarding Japan—observing it, considering it, comparing it. And I have been happily occupied; have learned much I would not otherwise have known. It could have been anyplace—even places I like better: Greece, Morocco. The results would have been much the same, since I did not remain where I was born.

But now I can see that I am getting older because there are waves of memory, a tide that wants to sweep me back to where I came from. This will not occur, but I must experience its effects.

I, who have spent my time meditating on difference, am now presented with "similarity"—what I experienced then and what I remember now. Forty-five years ago, Igor Stravinsky told me that at his age (which is what mine is now), he could for the first time remember the *smell* of the St. Petersburg snow of his childhood. Now, just today, out of nowhere, comes to me the sweet, watery taste of mulberries.

There was a tree in my aunt's garden, and I used to climb it to pick the white-and-purple fruit, to get it before the birds got it since, even back then, people did not much eat mulberries.

I remember the reason offered. The birds are fond of them, you see, I was told, and the seeds go right through them and so every tree is born from excrement and you don't want to eat that, do you?

I did not know then that many plants and trees thus grow, but I do remember seeing that this made a kind of dim bond between me and the mulberry tree, and that I ate more berries than ever. And now, suddenly, this remembered taste.

18 October 2002. In Japan, the incessant urge to aestheticize—everything, from tea ceremony to capital punishment. What this means is bringing everything to an extreme order, which is then presented, balanced, and regularized.

In the park I look at the homes of the homeless. Cardboard boxes precisely placed, a blue tarpaulin exactly draped. Inside, the found blanket folded as neatly as it would be at the Imperial Hotel. At one side a smaller box—this is for the shoes. The effect is not only utilitarian, it is also "beautiful"; that is, in accordance with the principles of good taste. And this from some anonymous builder who is completely severed from the common opinion he still represents.

30 November 2002. Fumio for dinner. His birthday, his fifty-third. We met when he was twenty. Now, passion long spent, we are good friends, meet every week or so, and take a selfless interest in each other. I ask about his daughter, Haruka, and he asks about Dae-Yung, the son who took his place.

Over our tandoori chicken he asks me if I was ever interested in someone my equal. Since this was in Japanese he could ask it, no matter how strange it now sounds in English. I suppose it could be translated to mean had I ever "fallen in love" with anyone with the same "general interests"; that is, caste/class. In any event the answer is no.

My interests are entirely in differences. The beloved other has to be all things I am not, though I might wish to have been. Dae-Yung, a soccer champ, not interested in books or movies, straight, much more interested in action than in cogitation.

I ask Fumio about himself. Oh, no, for him it is similarities that attract. His wife, for example. Or me. Now wait just a minute, I thought. How come

his difference attracted me, and my similarity attracted him?

As though I had said it aloud, he smiled, put down his fork and said, "Maybe I was not much like you at first, but I became like you. You had more influence on me than anyone else. You didn't see how much I had grown like you, and when you did we stopped making love and became friends instead."

I had not known that before.

4 December 2002. Ian calls from London. He is writing about me for *The New York Review of Books* and wonders how to handle the subject of homosexuality. Cannot leave it out, wonders how to put it in. So do I—I remember Auden: "A capacity for self-disclosure implies an equal capacity for self-concealment."

Possibilities: Not "gay"—gay is a lifestyle now, not a sex style. And not "queer," which I otherwise like, since it has now been taken over by academe. "Faggot" might be misunderstood, and "homosexual" is just too solemn, a po-faced word bristling with medical associations.

Ian does not want to use terms like "preferences," "lifestyles," etc., because they are euphemisms. Perhaps no word then. Words are half the trouble anyway. Instead, dramatize. He will think about how to do this, and I add that he might mention the *advantages* of homosexuality.

There is John Updike: "Perhaps the male homosexual, uncushioned as he is by society's circumambient encouragements, feels the isolated, disquieted human condition with special bleakness: he must

With Jim Jarmusch

man marked out by it the excellence of a separate condition. Consider the invert . . . he does not accept himself, constantly justifies himself, invents reasons, torn between shame and pride; yet—enthusiasts of the fatuities of procreation—we go with the herd."

1 March 2004. I rent a tape of *Tarzan, the Ape Man*, the 1932 version, the first with Johnny Weissmuller. I first viewed it when I was eight, and I now, next month eighty, want to discover if anything remains of what it was then. Expectant, I stared at the tube and remembered nothing at all about the story—except a bit about when the tribe of dwarfs throw the white people to the monster gorilla. What remained, however, what returned instantly recognizable after seventy years was the erotic atmosphere of Johnny and his jungle. The picture was made before the Hayes office was instituted, and Tarzan was mostly naked and Jane showed a lot of flesh too, and when he took her into his hut there was no doubt at all—even for an eight-year-old—what they did. What I had remembered and cherished for seven decades turns out not to have been elephants and crocodiles or even dwarfs. Rather, it is the loins of Tarzan, the naked hips hid barely by the loincloth. To be moved so at mere eight!

take it straight." A quote that means several things. Many men finally settle for the fact that they had children and this becomes why they are here—this is something that many women do, too. There is family life to sustain everyone except those who have never made families. In the end, the human condition wins out, to be sure. Maybe this is something that people with specialized roles know.

Later I look up another reference and fax it to Ian. It is from E. M. Cioran's *A Short History of Decay*. "Vice—bestower of solitude—offers the

I'm a silence so grim
No sparrow can flutter in
with his small music
Nor can a child's innocent rhyme
catch me
Where a wish grounds on bone

Acorn

Spas of the Mind

In 1963, Martin Berkovitz, a printmaker, draftsman, and painter, was living and working in Toronto. He and Milton Acorn were friends, and one night, depressed and down and out, Acorn asked Berkovitz (through a mutual friend) if he could sleep in his studio. Berkovitz agreed. At this time in his life, Acorn was in and out of psychiatric institutions and, on this occasion, had escaped from one of them.

That night as Berkovitz was dozing off, the glass door that separated his bedroom from his studio swung open to reveal Acorn standing in the dark, holding a knife. Not knowing if Acorn meant to do himself harm or what was going on, Berkovitz jumped out of bed and wrested the knife from him, and then took him to another mutual friend, who made arrangements for Acorn to be re-admitted into the hospital. When Berkovitz returned home, he found a poem scrawled on the wall of his studio. Berkovitz, who believes it was a suicide poem, was commissioned by Fiddlehead to do the drawing shown here (into which he incorporated the poem) for their Spring 1963 issue.

Mary Hooper, Milton Acorn's sister, on the People's Poet:

Milton could often be seen walking along the street or in a park carrying a scribbler under his arm, to be used at a moment's notice. It started as an ordinary school scribbler, but later grew to be an expensive hard-covered journal-type book. Some were priced as high as fifty dollars.

I believed that the bookstores deliberately lured him to them. I complained to Milton that he was paying their rent.

Now I realize that what is inside of the journals is much more valuable than the covers. Hundreds of them are in safekeeping at the Library and Archives Canada.

It is interesting to note that there is not a fingerprint on the pages. One might call them the Spas of His Mind.

Milton was always writing poems or bits of poems in strange places. I have several napkins from restaurants with his writings on them. I would not be surprised if he had written on some of the tablecloths if nothing else was available. He was always scribbling.

Falling to Grace

MICHAEL SILVERBLATT

Marilynne Robinson was born in Idaho in 1947, and has lived and taught in the United States and Europe. In 1981 she published her first novel, Housekeeping, *which won the PEN/Hemingway Award and was nominated for a Pulitzer Prize. Since then, she has published two works of non-fiction,* Mother Country *and* The Death of Adam, *a collection of essays. After a pause of twenty-three years, she has published her second novel,* Gilead, *a book-length letter told in the voice of the Reverend John Ames. In this letter, he tells his seven-year-old son about his faith, his experiences, and what came before them. The novel has been hailed as a masterpiece, has won the National Book Award, and just as* Brick *was going to press, was awarded the Pulitzer Prize. Robinson currently lives and teaches in Iowa.*

Michael Silverblatt spoke to Marilynne Robinson on Bookworm, *his venerable radio show about books and authors. The interview was originally broadcast in two parts on* KCRW, *Santa Monica, on March 17 and 24, 2005.*

MS: *Gilead* is a book written entirely in a state of intimacy and silence. Your narrator—the minister John Ames—is talking to his son, and there are things his son doesn't know that consequently elude the reader. So I first wanted to ask you if you could describe the intimacy of this novel?

MR: I think the question that focused the novel for me, that was central from the beginning, was the question of how one absolutely loved. And I thought of when a good parent has a child—their presence when they're with you as children makes you feel that under no circumstance could you ever cease to love them. Under no circumstance could you ever cease to forgive them. What they are is a fact of their existence and not a fact of any particular behaviour or attitude. This very pure understanding of the kind of sacred significance of another human being is something that can become attenuated or that you don't understand when you look outside your own relationships of that kind and see other people walking through the world misbehaving. So, there are two narratives going on. In one case, Ames is pondering the profundity of his love for his young son; on the other hand, he sees his dear old friend, Robert Boughton, struggling with his love for his own son, who's an adult, who's in his forties, and so it's that difference that Ames is imagining himself across. "I do not know you as an adult man. Whatever you are, I love you, I could never not love you."

MS: One of the things that the book surely convinces us of is that a minister is speaking. He knows his doctrine, he knows his scripture, he knows his theology, and he's a literate minister. He's read Karl Barth. He knows enough—he's speaking in 1956—to recommend that the people around him not bother with transgression, that they don't have to bring up André Gide's novel to him. [*laughter*] And yet, he's every bit as fallible as the son he hopes to instruct, and he even seems to want to instruct his son in his own fallibility.

MR: Yes, that is certainly true. He comes from a particular theological tradition, and one of the things that tradition assumes is that everyone is utterly fallible, but that's the human problem. It's as if there's a distance between what is true and what is humanly knowable, and there's a continuous struggle across these frontiers. So the sense of vision or revelation that would occur to him and be most important is precisely the discovery of his own error. But not error in a static sense; it's error as one half of a dynamic of realization, which is never final of course. It's never perfectly or even substantially correct itself.

MS: You've said in a lecture on narration that most fiction is about a character who comes to know his false relation to truth, to reality, to others, and that to a religious sensibility, this is the state of man in the world. A novelist writing about this is consciously replicating something sacred in that he's recreating the mystery of error that a human lives in.

MR: Yes, I think that's very true. And I think, to me, it's a beautiful idea because it sanctifies error. It removes guilt from error in a sense, because it allows for new discovery.

MS: Well, it also has a corollary—that all evidence is potentially false evidence. Most scientists would think of evidence as being the grounds for proof, but in the novel, as in God's world as imagined by the novel, all evidence is false in order to compel belief.

MR: I would like to hear you expand on that a little.

MS: We don't know we're looking at the world as a possible revelation, but what it reveals is something we have to believe in rather than have proven to us.

MR: Oh, yes, certainly, certainly. And I think that also, in the way that John Ames thinks, what is revealed is revealed in consciousness and not simply in outward experience, that what one can discover out of memory or out of misapprehension is also instructive. It's not a true–false dichotomy, but that there's a sort of manifestation of an aesthetic authority that makes meaning cohere.

MS: The present tense of this book is 1956. The narrator, seventy-six years old approximately, is writing a notebook for his seven-year-old son to read someday. In point of fact, the son today would be around fifty-one years old. And the father is writing the notebook because he has been told that he has a heart problem, angina pectoris, which, being a minister, has the cadence for him of *misera cordia*. So he is someone who takes what he's told by a doctor and hears in it the cadences of his vocation.

MR: Yes. [*laughter*]

MS: The narrator frequently says or fears that the pulpit is speaking in this notebook that he's keeping. Are there times when you feel, as a writer, that the under-structure is coming up from below?

MR: I felt so engrossed writing this book. I felt that I knew this character John Ames, and I was so mystified by him, because I thought I would write a book from a woman's point of view as I had done before. I thought I couldn't write from a man's point of view, and then suddenly here he was, telling me what he was telling me. I've never in my life, my odd life, had a stronger feeling of the actual presence of the character—like a self-induced delusion, you know, who knows all about *baseball*, what a surprise.

[*laughter*] There is the coincidence that he and I have many interests in common. He and I both belong to a tradition where speculative religious thought is perfectly respectable; it's very non-dogmatic. You can wonder all you want to within this large category. If I were preaching in that novel, the thing I would have been preaching is, "Isn't it beautiful? Look at water, look at light, isn't it beautiful?" I think that if there's any blessing I would want to put upon the world, it is that people understand where they are and what they're surrounded by, and the situation of the novel, let me ponder that and articulate it. . . .

MS: Only after I read *Gilead* and the essays in *The Death of Adam*, did I become aware that what I thought of as a mystical, lyrical, moon-maddened writer has a mind of great dexterity and power to persuade. *Gilead* is very sharp and logical and orderly. How does that mind write such miraculous air-chastened, light-glorified fiction?

MR: [*laughter*] It's an interesting thing. Truly, physiologically the experience of writing fiction is different from the experience of writing non-fiction for me. Both of them I love to do. I think that they nourish each other, but it truly is another mind. I mean, that's what it feels like. A bizarre thing to say.

MS: But do you think it is really? For instance, in *Housekeeping*, the girls go on a kind of night-sea journey across a lake, and they're going to come mysteriously to a kind of transcendental vision of creation, of the formation of crystals

and of fecund multiplication. I mean, it's an extraordinary vision that they have. In *Gilead*, the boy goes with his father, also on an expedition, this one a desert expedition in a drought, and he's going to have a vision that has to do with whether death is finality. The father, in this case, is trying to bury *his* father who won't stay buried, who lives beyond the grave in the life of the son. Nevertheless, this voyage occupies the same kind of role in both books. It seems to me meaningful that for the women it's water, for the men it's earth, and parched earth at that. Again, it seems that even if your mind is not operating on the surface in a knowing way, it's everywhere at work ordering and preparing a vision of the world that is very consistent.

MR: I think you're probably right. One of the things that I have been interested to do in my life is make a vision of the world that pleases me. You know what I mean? I feel as if I've been building and expanding my vision of the world. Sometimes I write it down, sometimes I don't, but it's very important to me. It is the central product of my life and anything else I produce is secondary. So it's not surprising to me that there is that kind of basic coherency in what I write, because it's what I believe. I would say as a statement of fact that reality is dazzling and that the capacity of human perception is dazzling, and that these things exist in a very profound and beautiful relationship with each other, and I think that the centrality of that conviction is so intense for me that anything I do will reflect it. It's what interests me; it's what I love, you know.

MS: One of the people who was at one point your teacher devoted an entire book to what he called the principles of design and debris. [*laughter*] That was John Hawkes. And it seems to me that your advance, or at least expansion, of that is that design and debris are *part* of one order, that they're not opposed to one another. And like truth and falsehood, they are part of God's order, and until we see them as part of a continuum, we're forced into a dualism that sees them as opposites. And the great marvel of your books is that whether the narrators know that or not, they inherit from you a sense of an expanded order that contains more than the divided consciousness of most narrators.

MR: I hope that's true. It certainly describes what I would hope for.

MS: How does that vision come about in you? It seems to me that, you know, with Thoreau, with Emerson, the poetic version of that vision is in the transcendentalist movement. Is that correct?

MR: I think you're exactly right. The nineteenth-century Americans are my great love. I took a wonderful American literature course in college with a brilliant professor, and I felt as if what was going on in that literature was so brilliant that I couldn't believe that it closed down. And I was quite conscious in *Housekeeping* of wishing to prove to myself the meaningfulness of that method, which is simply deep perception, and understanding experiences having endless and beautiful implication. I mean, everything finally being resolvable.

MS: It seemed to me in particular that Thoreau was of great importance because of the way words would move up and down in a manner that I can't quite explain, except to say that at their higher order they become emblems of something divine, and at the lower order they become puns, and they move up and down all the time throughout your narratives. How did you learn to word that perception?

MR: I don't know. I don't know how the mind learns. I mean, language comes before any kind of self-consciousness really. You're already adept as a young child, and who knows? One of the things that's so wonderful, I think, about writing is that you do have access to parts of your mind that you would never experience otherwise, and one of the things that you find out is that there's a massive amount of vocabulary, association, sensuous observation of a very close kind.

MS: I wondered whether either of these novels is meant by their author—I can speak for the reader—to provide a kind of conversion experience?

MR: To the extent that I could say that's true, what I want to convert people to is an appreciation of what they are and where they are. I consider that to be the first sacred understanding. What a mind is, what perception is, what the world is. What memory is. I mean, what a miraculous and strange, emotional thing memory is, and how it is the freight, it's the person. It's beautiful, it's amazing.

MS: But in the essays, for instance, you ask: "Why would you choose to be willing to live in a world that wants to deprive you of both sensual and spiritual comfort, and of cultural succour. Why would you accept this, without demur?"

MR: [*laughter*] I think that's a very live question and, of course, in my saying that I want to convert people to an appreciation of what they are and where they are, I'm saying that they lack those things, I think, in many cases. Somehow we culturally collaborate in depriving ourselves, and one another, of these most primary things. It's not as if people haven't always done this to themselves, you know. But at the same time, when you look back through the whole text of human experience, you can see there is so much that's beautiful and so much that's rich that we cannot look. It should accumulate for us like wealth, and in fact, we impoverish ourselves for no reason. For no reason.

MS: But reading your books, I come away with a feeling that in order to have these things back, God has to enter, and that this is the belief out of which these books are written. That these books are part of an argument whose answer is God.

MR: Well, I myself am, I think, very religious. I mean, in the sense that, as a deep, essential part of my sense of reality, I believe in God, not even knowing what the word means, you know. [*pause*] I suppose one of the reasons I hesitate to talk about it in a direct way is because this kind of language has been so cheapened, and I don't want to imply that I know what it means to believe in God. For example, I think that the *absence* that people feel can define God for them, you know what I mean? That to have the sense of lack or deprivation is to have the sense of the thing lacked. *Housekeeping* is about that to some extent. I think that if you assume you have control of these questions, that you know what it is to believe in God, that you know what God is, you are wrong. So that the people who are most believing and the people who perhaps think of themselves as not believing are probably much closer to each other, and then the people who truly are insensitive to the question are like the people on the other end who are totally confident that they have the answer.

MS: What you have in *Gilead* is three generations of American ministers. The first generation is the grandfather's. He is visionary, violently abolitionist, and he leads his congregation into the bloody Civil War. The second generation, that of the narrator's father, is adamantly pacifist. This preacher rejects his father's visions and his violence—he stops going to his father's church and goes to sit with the pacifist Quakers. Now our narrator, in 1956, is sort of a Hegelian synthesis of his forefathers. He has fallen into a state of uncertainty, although he is trying to teach his son about conviction. He has written thousands of pages of unpublished sermons whose theology boils down to an appreciation of transient and impermanent moments of beauty. He has turned from activism and from pacifism, and seems unaware that the country and the Church are on the cusp of a new movement, the Civil Rights movement. He seems to have fallen out of history.

MR: There's a way in which these three generations follow historical patterns. There were ministers who were very aggressive abolitionists, who went into the army, and who carried guns in the period during the Bleeding Kansas problem and so on. They were not intentionally violent—they weren't violent in the first instance—but there was so much violence that they became defensively violent as it were, and people overstepped the strictest definitions of defence and so on pretty readily. These are people, many of whom I admire in the sense that they gave up privileged places in New England or New York, who were so appalled by slavery that they felt that they could not excuse themselves from the problem. And slavery was terrible. It was an incredibly brutal, degrading institution, degrading to the people who were slave owners, as Jefferson and others have pointed out. Degrading to the whole society, and creeping into the North. It was not as if there was some clear line drawn. It was so economically important that it was undermining everything. So, I think that on the one hand if violence is ever justified, it was unusually justified in this instance. On the other hand, violence is horrible and repulsive and regrettable under any circumstance, and so there seem to me to be real questions for which there is no easy solution. I have real sympathy with the abolitionists and I have real sympathy with the reaction against the violence, but in the case of the reaction, it also erased every positive thing that the abolitionists were trying to accomplish. And that's history, and I consider it more inevitable than culpable in John Ames that he can't really sort those things out.

MS: He's part of this third generation and even though his friend Robert Boughton is not of the same ministry, they both have something of a fear of visions. Boughton says he doesn't know what he would do if he saw an angel, and our narrator, John Ames, says that although he knows and saw his grandfather having conversations and debates in the living room with the good Lord, he would be afraid of visions. So they seem to be of a generation that the grandfather has decried, that without visions there isn't a ministry.

MR: Again, historically, people like Ames's grandfather came out of the second great awakening in upstate New York and New England, and during that time—it's amazing to read about—typically they did have visions and the kind of vision that he describes is a fairly mild version of them, I mean in terms of the overwhelming character of them. And many people—like Charles Grandison Finney, who was one of the great abolitionists and first president of Oberlin College—had amazing visions of Jesus and they always said, "Go out there and free the slaves, what are you doing here?" And so, on the one hand, they took this incredible uncompromising energy from these visions; on the other hand, it gave them a kind of religious intensity that people after the crisis found pretty intolerable. John Ames is a Congregationalist and Boughton is Presbyterian, and those were two of the second-great-awakening abolitionist denominations.

MS: But it seems to me, here we have our narrator—the third that he knows of in a line of preachers, but he thinks that it can be safely assumed that there were several generations before—addressing his son on what may very well be his deathbed. And given the culture around him, he knows that this son is not going to choose the ministry. He knows it, not out of knowledge of *his* son—the son is only seven years old—but out of knowledge of sons; in other words, of the next generation. And if there's been some kind of history here, it's from a kind of fierce visionary religion to a religion that's more reasonable and pacifist to one that is reasonable and uncertain to a child whose values John cannot anticipate. People writing about John Ames regard him as a fount of love and certitude, and I find it very funny that in the book he is such a limited, uncertain character. Perhaps nowadays just hearing a voice of indecisiveness is calming and sweet—which may very well be the case—but he hardly seems the minister of great affirmation that readers seem to find in him.

MR: Well, when we were talking about vision before, one of the things that he wants to do is redefine the word, and what he's saying, in effect, is that many things are "vision." Memory is vision, subsequent realization can be vision. He also thinks in terms of sacrament, and he very much enlarges the concept of sacrament so that it comes in many forms . . . feeding the child casserole with a fork, and that sort of thing. [*laughter*] But in any case, it's not really consistent with his theology that he should feel that he has a final understanding. In other words, it's faith sustained in the sense of continuous process, continuous realization, rather than dogmatically, and so his own sense of his fallibility, which is a dogma for him, means that there are limits to the degree that he can insist or assert even. He loves, he earns love or discovers it, and this is theologically central, not any statement that he would make about it.

MS: Ames says that he doesn't know about the life his wife led before she came to him and that he's never asked her, and it seems a strange question not to ask and doubly strange because

he talks about hearing confession from all kinds of people. It seems strange in this book that certain things that you regard as open in the free flowing of understanding mutual spirits are in fact very difficult to speak of, so that he can't even speak to his friend Boughton about their mutual difficulty with Boughton's son Jack. Even that son, said to be something of a wastrel, has the devil's own time telling either of these ministers about a falling to grace that he seems to have had. Could you tell me about that silent communication? Is it something that's happened to them? Someone said to me, "Oh Michael, that's just Protestants!"

MR: [*laughter*] I think you're right. Well, in the case of Ames's wife, who is of course the boy's mother, he's an old reverend gentleman. He's not going to tell his son anything that would shadow his sense of his mother. So what he knows about her life or what she has told him, is not something that would be recorded for the boy, so that is open, but I assume that he knows more than he tells. As far as the situation with Boughton is concerned, to a certain extent I think you're describing culture there in the sense that there's a great deal of silent communication that occurs in certain cultures. My own family, for example. It is characteristic, I think, of certain groups of people that what is most present is least talked about, and it's not as if you're not acknowledging it and it's not as if you're not understanding it, but the acknowledgement and the understanding can take the form of silence.

MS: Could you begin to account for that? In my generation of Jews, when we've spoken to people who survived the Holocaust, it's felt that something will be lost if there is silence. So we have the pain of ongoing conversation about pain, and as a result, I find it difficult to imagine silence of the sort that's depicted in *Gilead*. Now, it is also a theology that asks us to believe that all those people were martyrs and that asks us not to think they were martyred to silence.

MR: In the relationship that Ames has with Boughton about the boy, he knows that Boughton knows there's a problem. He knows that he is, in effect, showing a certain disloyalty to this sort of father–son relationship that Boughten wished him to have with the boy if he does not seem to forgive him, seem to overlook it as his own father would do. So, in other words, what they're understanding in their silence is that they're honouring the relationship, that John Ames will not say, "Your son offends me" or "injures me," or "I'm alienated from him." That will not be said, even though they both understand the circumstance is one where, if they were not deep friends, it would be possible to say that.

MS: I would have thought that, on learning that Boughton's son has, in fact, learned how to be a good man, delivering this information to the dying father would be an act of grace. Instead, the book ends on an irresolution characteristic of this narrator, in that he doesn't feel that he has the right to risk bringing shocking, but happy and liberating, information to a dying man. This is mysterious to me, because I think in my tradition people go, "He's really a good guy, you don't have to worry about your . . ." [*laughter*]

MR: Well, you know, I don't like to give the ending away, but the fact is that the same "fall into grace," as you call it, is falling out of Jack Boughten's hands. This story is as sad as it is beautiful. I think if he were going to tell Robert Boughten the truth, he would be telling him something that would be as burdened with sadness as it is with grace. Is there "balm in *Gilead*"? Ought there to be? Yes. Is there? Another question.

MS: That's the other thing I wanted to ask you about, because as much as everyone knows "balm in *Gilead*," everyone forgets that the passage in

Jeremiah is one of the most war-torn, bloody statements from the implacable, magisterial, ferocious, stampeding Lord, you know the Lord who will not brook the oppressor.

MR: Right.

MS: And so it's very much a balm in the midst of a bloody, bloody fray. And the book seems to be about the consequences of that fray in every sense.

MR: Yes, and the consequences and the odd failure of those consequences. Which meant that an enormous price was paid and then the thing sought was not only lost but forgotten. I mean, 1956 is just the beginning of the Civil Rights movement, which really ought not to have had to happen if people could remember why they passed the Thirteenth, Fourteenth, and Fifteenth amendments.

MS: Now your core memory here is that the Midwestern ministers moved from the East to Kansas in the desire to make sure that Kansas and certain other states would not enter the union as slave states.

MR: Yes.

MS: And so their homes and their churches are thrown up in the midst of huge contention. You mention that the houses and churches were built not to become venerable, but in fact, to become shabby because they were contingent.

MR: Yes.

MS: There were churches that probably were not going to last and yet everyone stays and builds colleges.

MR: [*laughter*] Well, you know, one of the interesting things about the settlement of the Middle West is that these people, when they came out, did build colleges. It was one of the first things they were up to. Places like Oberlin and Grinnell and Knox College and Carleton College, and all these were founded typically by people from Yale or Andover or Amherst—one of that cluster of radical schools—and the idea was that they would create these colleges that were integrated and that admitted women, sometimes equally, sometimes in special little Barnard-style separate campus things, but in general, for the standards of the time, they were good feminists, you know. They had what was called the "manual labour system," which meant that everybody that came to the college did the work that was needed to keep the college running, which meant feeding the hogs and so on. Everybody did it; the president of the college did it. And some of these people who came out were extremely distinguished people in New England. People like Edward Beecher, who was the first president of Illinois College. These colleges were always on the Underground Railroad; they ran printing presses and so on. They printed so much abolitionist material that Southern postmasters would often just burn the mail rather than trying to sort out the abolitionist documents. But they would put up a college, teaching Greek and all that stuff, and then they would also build a church, because almost inevitably, these people who were starting the colleges were ministers. They would buy land from the government very cheaply, but when they built these institutions, it became very valuable land, relatively speaking, because people wanted to live around the colleges. So they could endow the college with the money that they made—the difference between what they'd spent on the land and what they sold it for—and then of course, this made little abolitionist communities, and then they would send students as missionaries out into the Middle West to preach abolition, which they did very effectively. So it was a whole system, a very ingeniously worked-out system, which had the effect not only of making sure that the slave economy didn't move into the Middle West, but also of preparing standards of social reform and social advance that were enormously forward-looking.

MS: You've talked about losing the lessons of the abolitionist movement. Is the present-day Church a participant in this decline?

MR: It's really . . . what should we say? It's not at the peak of its influence right now. The churches that were active in this way are what are now called the "mainline Protestant" churches, which have been pretty much marginalized—I hate to say that, maybe it's overstating—by this sort of more fundamentalist people, which is basically a kind of Southern style of religion. It's not New England; it's not upstate New York. These little schools have spun off; they don't have any religious identification anymore, almost all of them don't, so that, for example, at Oberlin, people have no idea who founded it or why. They don't know who it's named for. At Illinois College, they don't even

know that they're related to each other, that they have the same origins. This whole narrative is just gone and the culture that was created to stimulate and perpetuate reform has evaporated very substantially.

MS: One of the things that I find in the response to this book that annoys me is that it's presented as if the book were written for consolation, whereas I think the book was written out of a spirit of mourning for something lost. That it's really meant in the spirit of go thou and do likewise, if possible, and that what you believe in, you must find a way to maintain, which is what I believe both your novels are about.

MR: Absolutely.

MS: And that their extraordinary beauty is part of a magic spell by which the reader may be led to the recognition that what was lost is so beautiful that it's unbearable to leave it lost; in other words, these books are not meant to embrace complacency or nostalgia.

MR: Absolutely. I appreciate very much your statement of that. That certainly is my feeling.

MS: Could you speak about that? I mean, it's a sad thing to talk about—we're talking about the place we live.

MR: Yeah. Well, you know, I started reading about abolitionism, which I did because I was living in Iowa and I wanted to know where I was. Everybody will say, "Oh yes, my great-grandfather was in the Underground Railroad," but they don't notice or think about the whole implication of the fact that many towns were part of it, in many states. But in any case, it's the fact that this could've happened and could be forgotten, and that enormous setbacks occurred in terms of race relations and so on. In the fifties, people acted as if they were integrating colleges for the first time, as if it were a new idea. Utter erasure, and it makes you realize that history does not necessarily proceed in an orderly way. There are forces at work in it other than rational understanding or a coherent narrative, and many of the things that we think we have done and accomplished—like the public school systems, for example—are things that can be lost and swept away. Nothing that we have can be assumed. We have demonstrated a spectacular ability to lose precious things, and I think that that's really an important thing to understand right now.

MS: Well, I'm someone whose public school teacher taught him everything from the *commedia dell'arte* to binary math, and I mean by sixth grade. This was a time when a teacher was a person of wide aberrant wisdom, whose authority was total and who generated that authority by being fantastical, eccentric, wide-ranging, and respected. Now we have a generation of people who can claim the name *teacher* but not the respect that used to come with it.

MR: It's a tragedy. That's another thing, perhaps, that's lying behind the other passion that I was talking about—we are not willing to grant each other respect. This happens right across the culture. I mean, if anything can be said that demeans the value of any person or the work that he or she does, it will be said, and it will be taken as a more salient fact than any kind of accomplishment. I believe, deeply believe, utterly believe, that under all circumstances, the dignity of the human person must be honoured without any exceptions. You can understand the temptation to ridicule a criminal perhaps, but we don't limit it. It's like the whole culture is continuously looking for the opportunity.

MS: We ridicule sincerity, and the paradoxical thing about sincerity is that it's both ridiculed and prized. And so because the narrator of *Gilead* is sincere, critics think he's reliable.

MR: [*laughter*] Well, I do want to say for the sake of my good John Ames that he is unreliable in a world of unreliability, and that as somebody who observes and records his unreliability, he's in advance of most people, because we're all unreliable.

Unravelling Adriadne's Thread (with John Fowles)

PICO IYER

Dreams, Graham Greene believed—his last major book, published after his death, was a record of his dreams—come to us as much from the future as from the past. They exist in some untapped place into which we fall, for a moment, before recovering our usual position in life. Many of us, I'm sure, have had the slightly eerie sensation of reading a book describing events on June 23, and then looking up from the book at the calendar, to realize that today, in real life, is June 23. Or putting down a copy of Pascal to read a book by, say, Graham Greene, only to come upon someone picking up a copy of Pascal. The subconscious, as Pascal might have said, makes connections that reason cannot fathom: one reason, perhaps, why Greene read what he'd written every day before going to sleep, and woke up, he felt, with the answer to what sentence should come next.

Certain writers can perform a kind of fortune-telling—déjà vu in advance, as it were—almost naturally. Don DeLillo describes a toxic disturbance, and his novel *White Noise* comes out just as the Bhopal tragedy hits the headlines. Salman Rushdie describes a prophet pronouncing a curse on an apostate called Salman and . . . well, sadly, we all know the rest. This isn't a mysterious thing. These writers live so close to the world that they can tell, to some extent, what it will do next, just as we have a fair idea of what our friends or family will do next. Listen closely enough to someone and you become a kind of clairvoyant, or mind reader: the reason countries often had revolutions after Graham Greene was seen in them is that Greene was drawn to countries where he sensed a revolution imminent.

Yet there is another kind of correspondence—a telepathy between books, you could say—that is more curious, and is not explained at all by Harold Bloom, with his gnostic scholarship, saying that William Blake drew on Wallace Stevens. We read a book, and scarcely even remember reading it; and then, years later, find, perhaps, that we're living that book, or writing it—much as we dream, tonight, not of the people who fill our lives daily, but of those we might have met once, twenty years ago, in a café. They don't know us, we don't know them, and yet some odd kind of connection has been made.

In the summer of 2001, I completed a novel I'd been working on for years. It was a story of the clash—the romance—between Islam and the Western world, and it played out this theme by tracing a whole series of mysterious correspondences and synchronicities. A slightly priggish Englishman goes to California to study and teach Sufism, and there finds himself drawn into a maze-like web by a maddeningly elusive California girl with long fair hair, who claims to be an actress. Circling around both is a seraphic Iranian professor who may be manipulating them as a novelist does. The story is, in effect, about a quest into a labyrinth, and an arrival in a place where even the analytical scholar cannot begin to figure things out, and must surrender to what lies beyond his understanding.

The book behind me, I wanted to break into something completely different. A group in Washington invited me to take a trip to anywhere I wanted, and I chose Yemen: I'd long been drawn to the medieval land of tower houses and tribal kidnappers. I began to read up on the place and to gather my thoughts—and the project fell through. Then, two months later, an editor from Hong Kong called out of the blue. "You probably don't have the time," he began, "and you may not have heard of this remote place, but we're trying to find someone to go to Yemen. To retrace the steps of the fifteenth-century Chinese admiral Zheng He, who led his treasure ships and eunuch navies on seven journeys across Asia and the Middle East, and on two of them landed in Aden."

I instantly said yes, of course, and a few weeks later found myself in the small Yemeni port of Aden, where I had last been at the age of two, when it was the largest port in the world outside Manhattan. The hotel where I was staying was next to a beautiful harbour, where the USS *Cole* had been bombed by Islamic fundamentalists just nine months earlier. The area around which I drove was where Osama bin Laden and one of his wives had their home villages. I knew none of this at the time, though; all I did know was that, six weeks later, on September 12, 2001, I would send my book on Islam and its conflict with America to my editor.

I survived my stay in Yemen—and even a night-time drive across the country, through the mountains governed by tribal kidnappers—and decided, before returning to California, to spend a week in Greece. Like many a visitor to the Greek islands, I took with me copies of *The Names* by Don DeLillo, *The Colossus of Maroussi* by Henry Miller, and *The Magus* by John Fowles. I'd read all these books before—*The Magus* I'd only skimmed, looking for racy parts—and I wanted to see how they held up twenty years later. *The Names* was less magnetic than it had been, and Henry Miller a little less rapturous. As for *The Magus*, I got so caught up in the other two that I never got 'round to opening it.

But I'd bought a new edition of the famous Fowles book, complete with a new foreword by the author, so when I returned to California (the "Athens of the West," as the area was presented to me and my hopeful family when we arrived, in 1963), I decided to give it a try. Wild dry hills above me, and expansive, humbling blue skies; the sea foaming around rocks far below; and the sense, which is the promise of California (in my just-completed novel, and my life), of something pristine and even paradisal hidden within the hills and light, if only you can make it out. It was as perfect a setting as Santorini for delving into John Fowles.

The Magus, as most readers know, is about un-threading a long trail of clues and hints that lead deeper into a mystery that only leads into deeper mysteries. Yet what I found, reading it properly for the first time, is that it is, on its surface, about a somewhat priggish young Englishman going to teach on a rocky, sunlit Greek island, where he is led out of his complacency and away from his books by an elusive, fair-haired girl, who seems to be an actress. She leads him into the lair of Con-

chis, a kind of puppeteer, who delights in dabbling in Jungian games and thoughts of synchronicity. The Englishman, Nicholas Urfe, is pulled away from his girlfriend at home, away from the cozy life he knows, and toward something he can hardly fathom, by what he realizes are two English sisters, playing out some complex mythic plot. It was only after he finished writing the book, Fowles implied in his new foreword, that he realized how allegorical even the names (earth and conch) were. Readers are often drawn to the very books their own writers hardly care about, he says in the same foreword; for him, *The Magus* was just a young, unfinished project that had defeated him soon after he returned from two years' teaching on a Greek island. "A novel of adolescence," he put it rather harshly, "written by a retarded adolescent."

There were, I realized as I put the novel down, a few passing similarities between his book and the one that I had just finished writing. But that was not so surprising. Coming-of-age stories tend to follow a pattern, and if they concern themselves with educated Englishmen, they often include a liberation into a world of mystery and romance. Such books must be set in wild, sunny places—counter-Englands, as it were—and must be about being led away from old attachments and out of a world in which reason is king and everything can be explained away. From D. H. Lawrence to Lawrence Durrell, from Andrew Harvey to Alex Garland, the form is familiar enough to constitute a thriving genre. That Fowles centres his book on a pair of well-born sisters from Cambridge, that I included a pair of well-born sisters from Oxford (and another pair half from Oxford), was hardly something to marvel at.

Still, I was sufficiently intrigued by the correspondences—and taken with at least the first two hundred pages of *The Magus*—to turn to *Daniel Martin*, another book of Fowles's that had just been reissued in the same uniform edition. This was a famously recalcitrant work, inward and gnarled, that had lost Fowles many of his readers—in the twenty-five years since it came out, he had almost stopped writing novels, and instead retreated into seclusion in Lyme Regis, Dorset, to write odd, half-mystical texts about trees and islands and Stonehenge. *The Magus* had, in all senses, led the reader on, into mystery and myth, as if playing Ariadne's thread out into a labyrinth; *Daniel Martin*, by comparison, had all but turned its back on the reader to conduct a 629-page private investigation. Fowles's attitude toward his alter-ego protagonist was so vexed that he even switched back and forth between third person and first in mid-passage as if "alternately owning and disowning himself and his sins, both judge and accused in the court of his own conscience," as Adam Nicolson writes of a seventeenth-century Puritan shuttling between "my" and "thy" in his diary.

As it happened, I'd read *Daniel Martin* before—almost twenty-five years before—when I was just out of my teens and Fowles was a central literary figure. I'd heard about a new novel by the author of the cult book *The Magus*, who commuted between Oxford and California, as I did then, and was haunted by a sense of "Englishness" as only those in desperate flight from England could be. I'd recently come upon Fowles's own undergraduate book of aphorisms, *The Aristos*, and been impressed to find a figure of his class and education so ready to pursue the Other wherever it might lead him (to France, to Greece, even to a Jungian mage working through enigmatic girls); and so—for the first time in my life, I think—I had parted with a significant portion of my student allowance to buy a hardback copy of the book, and even written a long, quite unpublishable review of it. I could no longer remember a thing about the book, let alone my review; all that had stayed in my mind was an unforgettable trip to the rock-cut city of Petra, in Jordan, which had made such an impression on me that twenty-five years later and only months before I picked up *Daniel Martin* again, I had finally fulfilled a promise to myself by going there.

As I made my way through the intricate maze of *Daniel Martin*, I quickly found, of course, that it never goes to Petra at all, only to Palmyra in nearby Syria. This was, luckily, the one other historical site I'd seen on the way back from Petra. More than that, I could understand why *Daniel Martin* had been the last of Fowles's books I'd ever read. It was heavy with the self-doubt and riddlings of "male menopause," as Fowles calls it, with characteristic honesty, and where *The Magus* had been a sunlit frolic through the subconscious, *Daniel Martin* was more of a heavy-handed interrogation of it. *The Magus* was, in some sense, the mysterious stranger you meet on a summer holiday who takes away your heart (for a while); *Daniel Martin* was more like the old love, hedged with regrets and qualifications, whom you revisit years after you have drifted apart.

On its surface, the book tells the fairly conventional story of an Englishman who has prospered in Hollywood as a screenwriter, and who now begins to go back and forth between his life in Los Angeles (complete with much younger girlfriend—an actress, of course) and his memories of growing up in rural England and of the friends he made at Oxford. It allows its narrator—or its author—to draw the expected comparisons between the dream-life of L.A. after dark and the country roads of England, between the claims of worldly success and of integrity, between a culture of straight lines and one that is all corners and angles. And—as it was much easier for me to see at forty-four than at twenty—all this cuts with particular poignancy because the narrator has reached an age when the old, all that he has lost, weighs much more heavily on him than all that he might gain.

But what has always made *Daniel Martin* so difficult for a reader to like—*The Magus*, by comparison, is much too easy to fall in love with—is its sense of privacy and relentless self-analysis. Dispensing almost entirely with storytelling and incident, *Daniel Martin* has the sound of someone talking to himself at his desk, no longer concerned even about whether the reader is following him. In one of its most shocking moments, the screenwriter, turning on the people who support him, says, "Audience corrupts. Even more than power." There is a moment known to all of us when we look in the mirror and suddenly realize we're turning into the parent we've always tried to flee; *Daniel Martin* is possessed by this unease, and it hardly matters whether you call that parent Eng-

land, or formal religion, or just an actual old man.

So I could see why *Daniel Martin* had brought an end to Fowles's public career, in a sense. Indeed, it almost marked the beginning of his slow, silent passage out of our sight and into his stony cottage. Yet what was most haunting to me, rereading it, especially in the light of this valediction, was that *Daniel Martin* was, in tiny detail after tiny detail, the very book I'd just finished writing. *The Magus* had betrayed certain surface similarities to my novel; but *Daniel Martin* might almost have been its shadow or inner outline, not only in its pairs of sisters, its cross-questioning of skepticism, its search for a lost garden, and its sudden trip to New Mexico, but even in its cadences and most trifling moments. Again and again, I felt I knew what would come next, not because I'd read the book before (and forgotten it long since), but because I'd written it, as if by chance. Fowles's narrator says, in passing, that he's a "monk without a faith, or indeed even a monastery," and I recognized a sentence I'd confided to my commonplace book, more than once, several years ago. A man asks a woman, on arriving in a foreign place, how it strikes her, and I flinched because, although this is a natural enough question to ask in such a circumstance, my male character had asked my female character exactly the same question in exactly the same tone and phrase.

When I'd first encountered *Daniel Martin*, at twenty—and so eagerly written a review of it—my dream, for lack of anything better to do, was to become a literary critic; had I persisted in trying to achieve that goal, I no doubt could now have writ-

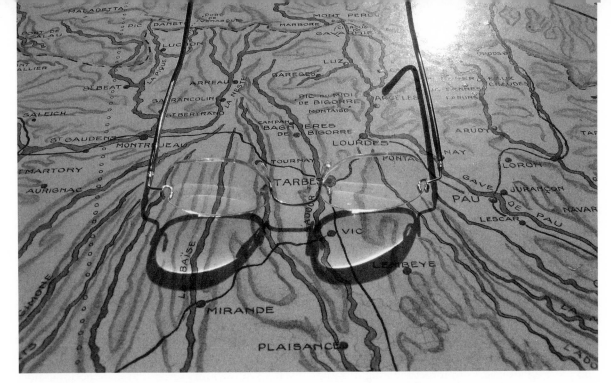

ten a learned treatise on the anxiety of influence, on the power of forgotten readings; I might have cited Borges's story "Pierre Menard," about a man who writes out much of Quixote, word for word, so exactly that it can seem that Cervantes was in fact drawing from him. But the theme of my just-completed book, *Abandon*, was precisely the sense that everything that matters in life, from love to mystery, sits outside easy explanations, and at some point we must let go of the rational structures with which we pretend to understand the world, and in fact hide from it. Things make a better, deeper sense than we can ever make of them.

In the quarter century since I first read *Daniel Martin*, I've read many, many books that have had a far deeper and more lasting influence on me; some have lodged themselves so fully inside me that I've read and reread them. And eight years of studying literature, followed by twenty years of reviewing books, have meant that many books have lived so close to me that they are a part of me and my life. But *Daniel Martin* was not one of them. When people asked me who had influenced my writing, I usually said, "Graham Greene," leaving them more perplexed than ever, since he was the one writer of whom they saw no traces in my work. I expected readers to liken *Abandon*, with its ringing of the changes on the one word of its title, its central tale of literary scholars trying to track down a hidden manuscript, and its long stretches of pastiche poetry, to A. S. Byatt's *Possession*, as they did. What I had forgotten—and they had too, perhaps—was that Byatt's novel was often linked, with its comparison of Victorian and contemporary love, and rhetoric of chivalry and the knightly quest, to an earlier book called *The French Lieutenant's Woman*, by John Fowles.

A stranger, coming upon the likenesses between my book and Fowles's, might have talked of plagiarism, or simply of that process whereby we take notes on a book, put the notes away, and retrieving them years later, think they are a record of our thoughts, and not of someone else's. But now, as a reader and sometime writer interested in the ways of the subconscious, I could see that life was rarely so simple and connections were seldom so linear. Many of the ways my book resembled his were too trivial to be anything more than coincidence ("I wouldn't have missed it for the world," says Fowles's woman, surprisingly, when finding herself in the Middle East; "I wouldn't have missed this for the world," says my female character, unexpectedly, when taken to Shiraz); others were too elaborate and precise ("You seem to forget the knight is just as much in distress as the damsel," Daniel Martin says, and the main character in my book not only makes the same point, but even uses the same high-flown imagery). You meet a stranger in the street and his way of brushing his hair back is somehow the same as yours.

What I was witnessing, I came to feel, was really more akin to a subset of friendship. You go to college, perhaps, at eighteen, and find yourself surrounded by new faces, in your class and dorm. Some of them become friends for life; some you never meet at all. Yet some of the most interesting connections are the ones you never quite make, with someone with whom you seem to share an affinity and yet never really get to know. Much as you meet someone for the first time and give her a book, and only ten years later realize that the book told the story of the friendship that developed between the two of you. This happened to me once. I thought of a friend I'd had in college, whom I'd spoken

to occasionally (about past-life regressions, in fact), but whom I'd never really got to know. Twenty years later, he came back into my life when I picked up a new novel in California and found that it was by him. I picked up the book, I think, because it was praised, on the cover, as the most interesting English novel encountered in several years, by one John Fowles.

The similarities between my recent book and some of Fowles's novels were not, I decided, the result of my reading his books so much as, curiously, the cause of my having read them in the first place. Something years ago had drawn me to a writer with whom I seemed to share nothing more than a background and a place of education. He didn't shake me, he didn't seem to be a person I wanted to be or write like, as many others did; but somehow he had certain habits of mind and interests—a language even—that turned out to be very similar to my own. It's easy to say we're formed by the books we read when young, but in certain ways, it seems that they are formed by us. We choose the books that are going to be unlikely friends.

Eighteen months later, my Islamic novel came out—though by that time the clash between Islam and the West was so much a matter of everyday discussion that what once had seemed a surprising subject might now seem quite stale—and my publishers, as publishers do, sent me to Canada to promote the book. I always relish trips to Canada because readers there are more alert and engaged than in any place I know (it's no coincidence that Canada has the most interesting writers I know, too); on a recent trip I'd even been interviewed by someone from my college magazine. This time, when I arrived in Toronto, I naturally picked up a copy of the grand institution you now hold in your hands, and found in it, amidst pieces on Apuleius and the musings of Cecily Moös, a long tribute to an almost forgotten novel, called *Daniel Martin*, by an admirer so possessed by it that he had made the long trek to Lyme Regis and actually caught a glimpse of the now-reclusive Fowles.

Two days later, a librarian from one of the local universities came to interview me and, as ever, asked me much more interesting and searching questions than I had got anywhere else (he had actually read my book twice). As he was about to leave, he asked, "Have you ever read a book called *The Magus*, by John Fowles?" "You've seen my publisher's catalogue," I said (in trying to make my book sellable, my publishers—for the first time in seven books and fifteen years—had, with no prompting from me, likened it to another work, the cult novel *The Magus*). "No," he said. "But certain similarities struck me. Like the fact that the main characters are near anagrams of one another." In my book, I'd consciously created two characters whose names almost contained one another, but I'd forgotten till now that part of the magic and mystery of *The Magus* is that "Nicholas" is almost "Alison," slightly rearranged.

"You never met Fowles?" he said, as we were standing up to leave.

"No," I said. Then, "Yes, I did, actually." I'd hardly thought of it till this moment—twenty-five years of other meetings and interviews had come

between. But suddenly I remembered that, as an eager teenager, keen to learn about the world of letters, I'd actually written to Fowles, asking if he would consent to an interview with the college magazine (the same one, in fact, whose writer had just interviewed me in Toronto). He, no doubt indulgent toward students from his own university and interested in literary matters, graciously said yes.

A friend and I had made the long trip to Lyme Regis, and Fowles kindly gave us lunch and then entertained us through the afternoon with tales of Hollywood, where he was then much in favour. He spoke of his plans, and of some of the curiosities of being a writer suddenly analyzed by critics. He asked us about our hopes, and I, no doubt, spoke of John Livingston Lowes's *The Road to Xanadu*, a book that consumed me in those days: the intoxicating story of a professor of Chaucer who, browsing in a library, finds a phrase that reminds him of something in Coleridge's dream-poem "Kubla Khan," then finds another phrase in an obscure fragment, and a fact somewhere else, and begins to undertake a journey through the poet's imagination, seeing how this phrase he might have met here and that detail he may have encountered there somehow coalesced in his sleeping, opium-haunted imagination to create the poem that came out of him when he awoke.

My friend and I, well pleased, returned to Oxford and wrote an entirely unintelligible piece about Fowles, likening him to Doris Lessing and Thomas Pynchon, not because he had anything to do with them, but mostly because we were proud of having read them. Yet what I remembered now—it had slipped my mind for all these years—is that Fowles had recalled something else that was interesting and that had piqued his curiosity as an occasional Jungian interested in the workings of the subconscious. A reader from Reading—the unconscious seems to savour such puns—had just written to him, he said, explaining how *The Magus* was in some ways just *Great Expectations* repeated. There was the same somewhat orphaned, slightly colourless young man at the centre; the cool, rather manipulative blonde woman who leads him into another universe; and Miss Havisham, orchestrating everything to make up for her own frustrations. Nicholas, Julie, and Conchis in profile.

The letter came as a surprise to him, Fowles said, since he hadn't been thinking of Dickens's novel at all while he was writing (though it was a favourite, and he had slipped an allusion to it into his first novel, *The Collector*). And I hadn't thought of it either till the librarian started asking me about Fowles, citing not the knotted, Jamesian book with which I had recently found such strong correspondences, but the quest-novel that had entranced so many of us in youth. Yet what was now strangest to me about the thought was that, in all my years of reading, only two characters had ever stolen my heart, though they had seemed among the least appealing of heroines. One was Estella, the cold, commanding girl in *Great Expectations*, who had recently come back to me via Gwyneth Paltrow's performance in the contemporary film. The other was a fair-haired girl, bewitching in part because so elusive and uncertain of motive, who slips in and out of view in a book I hadn't properly read till just now, called *The Magus*. We have a dream tonight and then, twenty, thirty years later, it becomes our life.

Sir Hardy Amies: Couturier to the Queen

MICHAEL ELCOCK

Sir Hardy Amies was the man who—until the early 1990s—designed the queen's hats, coats, and even her handbags. He died in March 2003.

In 1986, I was working on a novel that was built around some real-life events that had taken place in the summer and fall of 1944 in that little triangle of country where the borders of France, Belgium, and Luxembourg meet, at the southwestern edge of the Ardennes Forest. I was stuck for some necessary information about a little-known SOE (Special Operations Executive) mission with the code name of "Citronelle."

Brick readers may know that SOE was an "irregular" branch of Britain's secret services. It had been sanctioned by Winston Churchill, and it operated under the nominal control of Hugh Dalton, who—bypassing the heads of MI5 and MI6—reported directly to Churchill himself. Churchill's instructions to Dalton in 1940 were very simple: "Set Europe ablaze."

I knew that many SOE files had been destroyed in a fire at the SOE offices on London's Baker Street sometime around 1948, and that much information had been lost. However, I consulted all the texts I could find, including Cambridge professor F. H. Hinsley's exhaustive, and officially sanctioned, histories of Britain's secret wartime operations (*British Intelligence in the Second World War*). I conducted research in the U.K. and in Canada. But beyond the name of the operation and its commander (Bolladière), I was able to find very little information about Citronelle. In the end, I wrote to Professor M. R. D. Foot, the Oxford historian and biographer of SOE, to ask if he could help me find the information I wanted.

Professor Foot's reply, typed on a manual typewriter, contained some fascinating details about the operation. He told me that the operation was a disaster, and apologized for the paucity of the information he could offer. The group that was parachuted into Belgium, he wrote, was quickly cleaned up by the German SS. Foot's words, composed on a sheet of airmail paper—with typing errors and corrections and crossings-out—brought these long-ago events chillingly alive as I read them.

At the end of his letter, Dr. Foot astonished me with the suggestion that I contact Sir Hardy Amies, dressmaker to the queen—whom he indicated would know more about Citronelle than he did. He supplied me with the couturier's address, and so I dropped Sir Hardy a note with my questions about the operation.

In a couple of weeks, a heavily embossed envelope arrived in the mail, royal coat of arms and all. Sir Hardy's reply was polite, and answered none of my questions. But it was priceless nonetheless, Sir Hardy's tongue planted very firmly in his cheek. I think.

Dear Mr Elcock

It should not have taken so long for you to get an answer to your letter of 30 September ; it has only recently percolated through to me.

I am glad you have enjoyed my books on SOE ; but fear I can't offer you much useful help. Yes 'Citronelle' did work in the Ardennes, close to the Franco-Belgian border (and occasionally to-and-fro across it) ; but no, so far as I know it had nothing to do with the various Gestapo wireless games that had been operating - most of them in or near Brussels or Antwerp - for some long time before 'Citronelle' went in.

That mission's difficulties were due to something much more banal, a tactical accident. A survivor (now alas no longer accessible) told me that he and part of the mission were on one side of a thick hedge, while their companions were on the other ; their companions were caught suddenly by a Waffen-SS patrol, which never thought to find out whether anyone was on the far side of the hedge. Why one half of 'Citronelle' didn't try to rescue or to reinforce the other was left unstated ; reasonable I think to infer that the Waffen-SS were present in ominously great force, and the survivors thought themselves lucky to survive.

One of those captured was Hubble, till recently a GSO 3 (captain and staff officer) on the staff of the gaullist RF section in Baker Street. He was taken away to Buchenwald, where Yeo-Thomas - who of course knew him well - played chess with him, but was unable to save him from execution. The chess set they used is now, with a lot of Yeo-Thomas personal fragments, in the Imperial War Museum in London.

Your only source of information about what SOE was up to in Belgium is now a letter to the SOE Adviser, c/o Room E 203, Foreign & Commonwealth Office, London SW1A 2AH ; unless you care to write, ~~or something further~~ to Hardy Amies the queen's dress designer who was at once time head of SOE's T section, which worked into Belgium. 14 Savile Row London W1 is his business address.

I hope these jottings may be of some slight use.

Yours sincerely

Michael Foot

M R D Foot

BY APPOINTMENT
TO HER MAJESTY THE QUEEN
DRESSMAKERS
HARDY AMIES LIMITED

14, SAVILE ROW, W1X 2JN
01-734 2436

17th February 1986

M Elcock Esq.,
15 Manzer Road,
R.R.1,
Sooke,
British Columbia,
Canada.   VOX 1NO

Dear Mr Elcock,

   Thank you for your letter of 6th February. I regret
that I cannot in any way help you.

   I was in Brussels for the liberation celebrations
and remained there for nearly a year tidying up our work
with the Special Operations Executive. Some of these
celebrations did take place in the Ardennes but our visits
were short and occupied more with the people than with
scenery. I had nothing to do with military operations
as such. Our work was what is called clandestine.

Kind regards,

Yours sincerely,

Cassis

ROSALIND BRACKENBURY

In April 1952, Easter Saturday of that year, in Cassis in the South of France, my father went into the sea to save a woman from drowning. Another man went in, too, and was drowned. He was French, his name was Fabre, and he was an engineer from Marignane. Like my father, he was in his early forties and was married, with four young children. Like my father, he had served in the war. Like my father, he had come home safe, without being wounded or imprisoned. Unlike my father, he was not a strong swimmer.

It was out at one of the *calanques*, called Sormiou, a few miles west of the town of Cassis. My mother, who saw what was happening, hitched a ride on a motor bicycle back into town to raise the alarm. The boat had already set out from the port. They found the young woman and the body of the other man. Nobody had seen my father. The third swimmer, *le troisième nageur*, was missing and was thought to have drowned. My mother made them go out again. The boat turning, its wide wake. The choppy sea. This time, they brought him in.

I knew nothing about this, until after my father's death in 1991. Then I found the newspaper yellowed in a desk drawer. Nearly forty years, a story lying in a drawer. As soon as someone dies, you begin opening drawers. And there they lie, the artefacts, the signs of life.

Le Provençal d'Aubagne, le plus grand quotidien du Midi, Monday, April 14, 1952. The headline: A man drowns at Cassis trying to save a young woman. And the sub-headline: A third rescuer: an English tourist comes to the help of the *malheureux en perdition*. DRAMA OF SEA RESCUE AT CASSIS. And then, today slightly cloudy skies, likelihood of storms in the afternoon. One hundred thousand tourists on the Côte d'Azur for Easter. Van Steenbergen wins the Paris–Roubaix cycle race. The thieves of the yacht *Rodeo* escape the police. A young woman, Marie Raymond, may have poisoned twenty people. Two trains crash into each other in the Gironde. The lion tamer Fredo Menzano was attacked by the lioness Rachel. Thirteen dead, twenty-three wounded in road accidents. And on page five (*suite*), the third swimmer was invisible and was thought to have drowned. But this was not the case.

The cave later known as la Grotte Cosquer, was discovered by Henri Cosquer of the Cassis Diving Club in 1985. Cosquer did not announce its existence to Maritime Affairs in Marseille until 1992, after two Norwegian divers had died there in 1991. The cave is about twenty thousand years old, according to carbon dating of the charcoal used in drawings on its walls, and is reached by a narrow tunnel 175 metres long, and is entered at a depth of 37 metres. A second, shorter tunnel leads to a tall, high-ceilinged chamber known as la Cathédrale and a deep well. In section, the whole cave resembles a woman's reproductive system. The paintings on its walls include imprints of human hands, horses, and marine animals, such as penguins, seals and fish, which would have existed in the cold climate of Provence twenty thousand years ago.

On July 31, 1944, a plane disappeared into the Mediterranean, into the waters off Cassis. The pilot was Antoine de Saint-Exupéry, and he had left the aerodome at Borgo in Corsica to fly a reconnaissance mission over occupied France. It was his last mission.

It was 8 A.M. when he left Borgo, twenty-five kilometres from Bastia. The night before, he'd arrived in town in a Jeep. That evening, he'd had din-

ner and a bottle of wine in a restaurant in Bastia. His bed had not been slept in, and nobody was really expecting him to show up; another pilot had been designated as a replacement. But at dawn he ate in the mess—fried eggs, coffee, American cigarettes—and by eight, he was off the ground, heading toward the French coast, with only a camera on board, to undertake an aerial reconnaissance at high altitude between Grenoble, Annecy and Chambéry. He was forty-four years old, at a time when a pilot was considered old at thirty. He was a risk taker, had flown all night across the deserts of North Africa, carrying the mail, alone with the stars.

"Surely, Captain, you aren't expecting to be still alive after the war." It was Saint-Ex's friend General René Gavoille who said this, during the Battle of France. Later the general called on him at his villa at Cap Corse and warned him that the planes the Americans were letting the French use, the P-38s, were like ruined thoroughbred horses, spoiled, worn out, not fit to fly; delivered at the last minute, without either instructors or instructions—one had cost the life of a pilot only days earlier, with a fire on board and an oxygen mask that didn't work. His friend said later that he'd wanted to tell Saint-Ex the date of the projected Allied invasion from North Africa, so that he wouldn't fly and risk falling into Nazi hands. But Saint-Ex had given up honours, fame, a New York apartment and life as a writer, to come back here and fly the ruined thoroughbred, whose prototype he had already crashed into an olive grove.

It was, anyway, to be his last mission. At 3 P.M., in Borgo, René Gavoille paced, checking his watch.

Half an hour later he knew that the P-38 had disappeared. "Photo mission at high altitude over the South of France. No return."

During the war, eleven thousand Allied planes had been shot down over France. More than five hundred of them were downed over Provence or the sea offshore between November 1943 and 1945. But that July morning, the Germans had not brought down a single plane in the region.

How can a plane fall from the sky, from ten kilometres up?

"J'aurai l'air d'être mort et ce ne sera pas vrai," Saint-Ex had written of his flights over the desert. "I will appear to be dead, but it will not be true." What can he have meant?

Silence.

Then on September 7, 1998, a fisherman called Habib Benamor, born in Tunisia, was trawling in deep water off Cassis, near the Île de Riou, and brought up something shining in among the fish and weed and didn't throw it back. His boss, Jean-Claude Bianco took a look at it, cleaned it and found the inscription: Antoine de Saint-Exupéry (Consuelo)–c/o Reynal & Hitchcock, Inc.–386 4th Ave., N.Y. City–U.S.A.

It was Saint-Exupéry's identity bracelet, given to him by his wife Consuelo, with the address of the American publishers of *Le Petit Prince*. His Consuelo had had it made for him specially. Because she wanted to keep him safe.

These three things all occurred in the same place. Different men, at different times, for different reasons, go down into the same piece of water. What

links them? Not causality. The stories can't be linked by cause and effect in the normal way. Is there a synchronicity of place? Archaeologists know that finds are made in certain places because these are the places where archaeologists are looking. Turkey, for instance, or Israel some years ago. There appear to be no Neanderthal remains in Afghanistan simply because nobody has been able to dig in Afghanistan for so long. Politics dictate where one can, or cannot, dig; geology shows where one should dig, if possible.

The politics of today are that the Second World War is over and it is possible to go to the South of France, where once beaches were mined and booby-trapped. Where parachutists floated down onto sharpened posts set at angles in the dark.

The war runs through this story like a taut thread. The silences of that generation, governed by secrecy. The way both M. Fabre and my father had been trained to try to save lives. The Allied landings made in 1945 from Corsica on the southern coast of France.

The geology is what has been slowly evolving for twenty thousand years, since the Grotte Cosquer was a land cave, not filled with water.

Two men died in the Grotte Cosquer before it was made known to the public. Consuelo, Saint-Exupéry's wife, was left widowed, as my mother could have been. *La petite rose* of *Le Petit Prince* never knew what had happened to Saint-Ex. Until the bracelet was found, neither did anyone else. A vanished writer. A cave full of vanished animals. The vanished, or hidden, account of my father's heroic act, in a desk drawer out of sight.

I was looking in the South of France, excavating Cassis, because of the way my parents pronounced that one word. Because of the look they exchanged when they spoke it. Secrets draw one to their hiding places, they lie in wait for decades. But the magnetic pull of their presence is there, whether or not they are known.

Dark blue water slops against the bow of the boat, white water fans out behind us in a long V of wake. The boat's painted bright blue and a man in a dark sweater is at the tiller. The engine carries us fast, slap slap into the waves. I see how the currents cross each other out here and how the wind churns up the water in a few moments.

We're heading out towards the *calanques*, and the cliffs are striated horizontally, grey granite. The sky is a cold blue. It's spring again, but this time it's fifty years later. Spring 2002. We head straight out to sea, then turn into the first inlet, the Calanque de Port-Miou. Then there's Port-Pin, d'En-Vau, Morgiou and Sormiou. In and out, with the sea whipping around us, a stiff breeze, the water dark blue, almost purple where it goes deep. Waves slap the bow, the engine churns up white like liquid marble as the boat turns.

At the farthest, the Calanque de Sormiou, a woman is clinging to a cliff, with a child clinging to her. She cries out to us to help her, and the captain turns the bow, slows the engine, motors in sideways to pick her off.

"Does this happen often?" I ask him. "People getting into trouble out here?"

"You would be amazed, Madame. People who climb the cliffs and can't get down, people whose boats capsize, swimmers who are caught by the current, people picnicking on rocks who don't notice that the tide has come in. Luckily for them, we are out here a lot, taking tours; or the Marins-Pompiers would be busy."

The child, a little girl of about five, howls once she has been rescued. Her mother seems distracted still, fusses around the captain.

"Ce n'est rien, Madame. But another time," he adds, "it would be better to pay attention."

The woman's damp skirt clings to her legs. Her feet are white and arched, with a long smear of blood from a cut. Her daughter sobs, perhaps with relief.

Was it here? Was this the place?

I can't be sure. Yes, this farthest inlet, the Calanque de Sormiou, where the woman was clinging to the cliff must be the one. But you can't say *this* is the place. There are so many *calanques*, these sharp inlets running inland under cliffs, rocky places where the sea at high tide rushes up into the crevices, covers the rocks. So many places where a person could drown.

This must have been the way they came back, anyway.

We're in the channel where the boat carried my father back into port fifty years ago; and nothing more can be known about that journey, that crucial forty-five minutes, than is already known. The water is as deep as ever. Hundreds of accidents happen here, hundreds of rescues take place.

What takes over is the present, today's emergencies, today's concerns.

I can see the approaching port, though, the lighthouse at the end of the stone quay, the place where the boats turn to come into the harbour, the line of bars and shops along the quay, the houses massed behind them, the umbrella pines on rocks on the port side, and to the starboard, far off, the long rise and sharp drop of Cap Canaille. This is where, this is how, they brought my father in. It matters, to be here.

Nothing just takes place on the inside, between people; the third thing, the base line of the triangle, is the place, the exact spot on this earth. Or in the sea, underwater, in invisible tunnels and caves.

Or in the air. There are places, simply, where life streams through and condenses, because of what has happened there, where the current of it runs fast and deep.

They found the wreck of Saint-Exupéry's plane in September 2003; or rather, they found part of it. It was all in the papers, *Le Monde, Le Nouvel Observateur.*

"Je finirai en croix dans la Méditerranée," he had written years before. And now, in this new century, sixty metres down, to the north-east of the Île de Riou, part of the wreck of the plane was pulled

up from the sea bottom, without any bullet marks on it or signs of an explosion, only the kind of damage that would have been made by a plane coming down into water at eight hundred kilometres an hour. The man who was the chief at Géocéan, an underwater exploration company in Aubagne, who grew up with a model of the P-38 on his bedside table, who dreamed of an alchemical link between man, sea, and plane, was one of the men it took to find the wreck. Another was Henri Delauze, a businessman and retired deep-sea diver. Between them, they were to spend a good million euros on the exploration. Then there was Luc Vanrell, diver and wreck specialist, who remembered once having glimpsed a strange heap of rusted metal one kilometre north-east of the Île de Riou. And Philippe Castellano, amateur historian and diver, who spent months deciphering the hieroglyphics of the number hand-stamped on the fuselage. Mechanics, businessmen, historians, fishermen, divers— all crazy, you might say, to have devoted so much time, money, energy, and sheer passion to the search. But it was what it took to find it, and be sure.

The rest was detail. A failure of oxygen that made the pilot lose consciousness, a huge engine out of control, a pilot who pushed the plane's nose up for one last time into the blue, in the deserts of the sky. And fell. A writer plummeting wordless and unseen into the depths of the sea.

For me, it was a yellowed copy of a newspaper, found in a drawer: *Le Provençal* for that day in April—Easter—in the middle of the last century, when an Englishman had gone to the rescue of two people who were drowning, and had been pulled up nearly lifeless himself from that same sea.

A thousand tourists on the Côte d'Azur, that day in April. Van Steenbergen won the Paris-Roubaix cycling race. Did Marie Raymond poison twenty people? Two trains ran into each other in the Gironde. The lion tamer Fredo Menzano was wounded once again by the lioness Rachel. And a woman was saved from drowning.

It was a postcard, a black and white photograph of fishing boats in the port of Cassis, with a crinkled edge, a blurred but legible postmark and a message in slanting writing, "To thank you and remind you of the place in which you have been so brave."

Tale of the Bong

VASCO RAY

Pygmy music is what brought me to the Central African Republic eighteen years ago. Well, maybe not music only. A two-year magic mushroom binge may have played a role, too. Twenty years ago, I lived in a trailer in a remote part of Scotland. In early fall, these cute little mushrooms, "liberty caps" the locals called them, popped up in pastures up and down the valley. When I first began eating them, they weren't too easy to come by, but I developed an eye for spotting them and had usually collected a decent handful after an hour's forage. Then the liberty caps responded to my attention in a dramatic way. They became more and more plentiful. In the beginning, I had to search for them in distant pastures. But soon they were bursting out of the ground in clumps around my trailer, where locals claimed they'd never seen them before. Hundreds of them, then thousands, then tens of thousands. Sometimes I crawled around on all fours and grazed on them like a sheep. I strung them up to dry so that I could eat them every day throughout the year.

I didn't stop eating them for two years. I became increasingly aware of something trying to make contact with me. This something turned out to be—I'm not kidding—an extraterrestrial intelligence that had inhabited this earth far longer than we humans. It gave me clear instructions: go live with the Pygmies. Go. So as soon as my head cleared, I went.

The Pygmies are called by many names, as they themselves like to point out. In Congo and the Central African Republic (my stomping grounds) they're called BaBinga or BaMbinga, Beka, citizens, and of course, *les pygmées*, a name that dates back to Homer. Two thousand years before him, the Egyptians called them Akka, which sounds closer to the names many of them call themselves today: Biaka, Bayaka, Baka, Akoa, Asua, Twa. The people I live with call themselves BaAka. Little is known for certain about their history, other than that they've been around for a *very* long time.

I'd heard about the BaAka's fondness for cannabis before I ever visited them, and in fact, it was this fondness for the sacred herb—coupled with the probability that if they were so fond of it, it must be readily available—that made a prolonged sojourn among them a prospect I could seriously contemplate.

The Aka word for marijuana is *djama*. But the BaAka are always coming up with code words to enable them to speak about *djama* even in front of the police or gendarmes. There's *makoota, maboonga, mosh,* and a host of other more ephemeral terms I've forgotten. They call it *eye medicine*—often shortened to *eye*—because of its ability to help them see things differently. When asking for grass, they may call it *crap* or *bullshit* to indicate they'll be happy even with pot of the poorest quality. It becomes *little* when what they mean is any quantity of reefer, however small. *Spinach* is your run-of-the-mill, inferior-quality weed. *Rat shit* comes from the dried mouse or rat turds that often turn up in the little round paper-wrapped packets of marijuana that sell for twenty cents each. After a visit to northern Congo, I returned with more slang: *red duiker* and *blue duiker,* the two most commonly caught forest animals (i.e., something good to be divided up and shared out, as meat is). At my village these two words quickly spawned others: *porcupine* and *squirrel* and *forest rat* (to name but a few), prompting exchanges like, "Got any red duiker today?" "Nope, all I've got is a little leg of squirrel."

It wasn't long after my arrival in the Aka village of K——, where I still live today, that I was sharing spliffs with the young men. Like Europeans, BaAka in the Central African Republic prefer to adulterate their herb with tobacco, a preference that I (coming from several years' residence in Europe) shared. (Only later, when I went to Congo, did I find BaAka who smoked their herb straight.) They smoke this blend in roll-ups. Traditionally, the leaf of a common undergrowth shrub served as rolling paper, giving each toke a sweet, autumnal taste. But the younger generation was already switching to paper when I arrived, and used almost any scrap they could lay their hands on, however toxic it might appear to be. They used the brown paper from paper bags; they used the thin sheet of paper, covered in elegantly printed instructions in five different writing systems, that came with the local tiger balm (also my paper of choice whenever I ran out of Rizla or Zig-Zag); they were adroit at peeling a thin inner layer off cigarette cartons for a superior-quality paper; in a real fix, they might even resort to a page from a magazine, though as a rule they avoided paper that was glossy or printed with colour photographs. They liked their rolling paper stiff, which is why they always declined my offers of genuine Zig-Zags—just as well from my point of view, since for years there were no rolling papers for sale in the entire country.

In those days, I mixed tobacco with pot and was entirely at home with the BaAka's smoking habits, the only significant difference in habit being that a joint once passed is never returned. You smoked until you were satisfied and passed it on. I spent

many pleasant hours with the young men in this fashion. They came around to brew up sweet weak coffee on my fire and to smoke my cigarettes and cannabis. I enjoyed sitting with them, getting to know the various characters, listening to their conversations, of which I rarely understood a word. Only one thing bothered me: so far, my contact was with young men only. The elders showed no inclination to linger once they'd gotten a cigarette or some weed off me. I gathered they regarded the smoking of joints as kid's play. They smoked their reefer in a big bamboo bong. Before long, I decided that if I ever hoped to be included in their company, I'd have to join them in their bong-smoking ceremony.

At that time, the village of K—— had two bongs of renown. One belonged to Mobo, a little guy, but deadly with a crossbow, who had once been ambushed by a leopard that he managed to kill with his bare hands. He still bore a deep gash across the top of his skull. The other bong belonged to a fierce elder named Diboko. Both were known to cause smokers to pass out.

I quickly established a routine which became, degree by degree, all-consuming. Around nine each morning, my pockets packed with pot, a pack of fags tucked into my sock, I would arrive at Mobo's home—an airy hemisphere of sticks shingled with large oval leaves—and call out his name.

If he was around, which he usually was, since increasingly he knew what to expect, he emerged from the darkness inside, face dimpled by a smile of anticipation. We were about to embark on his favourite leisure activity. Together we repaired to a pleasant shady area in a secondary forest, the usual site of our bong sessions. Several other adult men from the neighbourhood, not all of them elders, would be on their way over to join us.

The *mokoondu* is not, strictly speaking, a bong, but it's even less a pipe. Lips are placed inside its wide opening to draw in the smoke, but instead of passing through water, the smoke goes through a fluffy mass of wood shavings that have been soaked with water. The preparation of this stuffing, *moosimbu*, for the bong's bamboo chamber was itself something of a fetish for the bong owner. Mobo always insisted on adding fresh *moosimbu* to what was already in the bong. Conversation ran rampant as he scraped on a branch with his knife. All the usual faces were there: cranky Simbu and his inarticulate but sweet-natured son-in-law Esimba; Maboongi, "the mayor," not yet the grand wise elder he'd one day become; old Dombi with his nearly infrasonic voice. A sample of my latest score would make the rounds, prompting much happy commentary by this panel of experts.

Meanwhile, Mobo's preparation of the bong would be nearly complete. Fresh water was poured through and soaked up by the *moosimbu*. Airflow through the bong was duly tested and deemed acceptable. The bowl was amply filled with a blend of marijuana and tobacco. The ritual could begin.

As bong owner, it was Mobo's prerogative to stoke it and enjoy the first lung-busting hit. This was the great moment at last. Everybody watched as he picked up small glowing pieces of charcoal in his bare hand and crushed them into the bowl. The simple expedient of matches or a lighter was scorned by all. Working his cheeks like a bellows, Mobo huffed and puffed until the temperature in the bowl reached the critical threshold. Sparks shot out and embers burst into flame as he reaped his reward: a long and powerful toke.

My turn always came next, my right as the supplier—a right I was rarely willing to surrender. After me, the bong might be good for two more substantial hits. Depending on the number of men present, we smoked anywhere from two to eight bongs, until everyone had come third in line at least once.

Having passed one or two hours in this agreeable manner, I would leave my friends to their repose and stroll to Diboko's at the other end of the village. I invariably found him waiting for me, bong at the ready. Although each bong had its regulars, some men frequented both. But never did Diboko smoke Mobo's bong, or vice versa. The very idea seemed unthinkable. Hence, a visit to Mobo's always had to be followed by a visit to Diboko's. Not that I minded the obligation in the least. Diboko's bong was the ultimate *mokoondu* experience. If you smoked it just right, it launched you into that sweet zone between bliss and unconsciousness. Many a time have I wobbled there, and had water poured over my head from the pitcher always on hand. *Poor Mobo,* I sometimes thought, *bound by custom never to experience this!*

The different crowd at Diboko's included his older brother Djolo, a skilled tooth extractor, and Wasili, who shared many grandchildren with Diboko. We smoked the hour away, the same formula at work, until I determined that everybody present had been well accommodated. And then—then it was time to return to Mobo's, and start the cycle all over again.

Those were days I could never forget. Conversations and storytelling became de facto language lessons for me. Lifelong friendships were forged in the smoke of the bong. For the first time, the elders began to consider me someone worthy enough to take with them into the forest. I looked back on my days of sitting around the coffee fire sharing joints with "kids" as a sort of dark age. Those "kids" befriended everybody. But the elders represented a more exclusive company. They were picky in their choice of company. Admittedly, I'd given them a powerful incentive to choose me, but once they did, we became genuine friends. And what further proof could I ask than this: whenever the elders scored something to smoke, they started to invite me to smoke it with them.

Eventually, however, I couldn't help but realize that I'd become the biggest, baddest bong bum in the village. Scarcely a session was held where I wasn't present and accounted for, and at full attention. Duty alone required me to smoke ten bongs a day just to maintain the equality between Mobo and Diboko. And then there were all those friendly invitations, those freebies as I thought of them. Hard to turn down a freebie when I knew what a privilege such an invitation represented. Even when

I was shaken awake in the middle of the night to share a nightcap, how could I fail to respond to such generosity, such thoughtfulness, with anything less than prompt participation?

But gradually a problem arose: something was awry with my eyes. I found that it required increasing effort of will to focus on anything, and even when this focus had been achieved, the object in question remained in a halo of blur. At first I blamed this blurring on lack of sleep, but soon I discovered that the problem lay in one eye only. Whereas my right eye remained as sharp as ever, my left had developed an extremely annoying twitch, a vibration of the eyeball itself, which rendered anything I looked at a blur. In fact, as the weeks and then months were swallowed up in one big pungent cloud of bong smoke, I realized that I could improve my sight considerably by the simple expedient of wearing an eye patch. With my right eye alone, my vision regained something of its former acuity. Soon the patch became a permanent feature of my face. My Aka friends, mildly concerned at this turn of events, asked me what was wrong. "Oh, nothing serious," I'd reply, making light of the matter. "My left eye just doesn't work anymore. But don't worry," I'd continue as I raised the bong to my lips for the eleventh time that day, "I've still got my right."

One night, after a particularly vigorous smoke-up at Diboko's, I was on my way back to my house—a small lean-to made from plywood shavings scavenged from the lumberyard—when I paused to look up at the stars. The sight of the stars has always awed me, but it was a sight I rarely treated myself to these days, because stargazing had been a lot more fun with two eyes. I believe the star that caught my attention that night was Betelgeuse. Out of curiosity, I removed my patch for a peek at it with my left eye. But my left eye saw no star, only a blur of light that darted about like a UFO. And suddenly, it dawned on me that my malfunctioning eye might not be unconnected to my career as bongmeister.

So did my bong-smoking days come to an abrupt, albeit reluctant, end. I would go on to regain the use of my left eye, and to have a lifetime of experiences with the BaAka, but never again would I recapture that special rapport I shared with the elders when our common purpose was but to keep the bamboo bong smoking.

Afterword

It's interesting to compare the effects of cannabis, which is illegal, with those of alcohol, which is legal. The clarity of this contrast is striking.

Take fights. In twenty years of visiting the BaAka, I've never witnessed a single fight fuelled by cannabis. Alcohol, on the other hand, in all its forms but particularly the popular moonshine distilled from corn by the BaAka's villager neighbours, is a powerful catalyst of fistic discord. As if by magic, fights proliferate out of nothing. Often, the two initial combatants are drinking buddies returning from a binge. If the consumption has been more widespread—after payday at the sawmill, or one of the large cash deliveries the BaAka extort from me from time to time—then the fight risks becoming epic, like a battle out of the *Iliad*, complete with spears and large logs of firewood, many of them ablaze. First to be co-opted into the fray is usually the well-meaning but hopelessly drunk self-appointed mediator. Very often, this mediator, dancing like a hyperactive referee between two pugilistic opponents, was the third drinking companion. Like Larry of the Three Stooges, the mediator is the one who usually ends up with the most serious injuries. At first commendably neutral, something—usually a misplaced blow from one of the fighters—will inevitably turn him into an antagonist with a strong partisan bias. This two-against-one state of affairs never lasts long. Out of the ranks of the spectators, a relative of the mediator's opponent now throws in his lot, evening out the odds. Spin-off fights are common. Occasionally, one of these will even develop into the main conflict, supplanting the original fight.

A main variation on the fight theme is battle between husband and wife. These fights don't always turn out as dreadfully as one might fear, as usually only the man is drunk and therefore not particularly fast on his feet, and Aka women, though normally smaller than the men, are very strong. Also, they don't hesitate to escalate the conflict with a pre-emptive strike with a machete or a block of blazing firewood. Frequently, this brings the fight to an abrupt end.

And the bad effects of cannabis? Well, certainly there's the physical nastiness of inhaling all that smoke. Too great an overindulgence, however, generally leads to nothing more serious than a nap. Music making is a popular activity that goes along with smoking reefer, much as fighting goes along with the consumption of alcohol. Other times, as in any university dorm, this gentle weed of awakening inspires debate and armchair inquiry. In which direction is the end of the earth? Where does God live, if not in the heart? Did you ever see a ghost?

I admit that now and then, a cannabis casualty comes along, some boy who gets too fond of cannabis and turns into a loafer and expert moocher of roaches. The community targets these cases with relentless ridicule, and most boys eventually grow out of this phase and become active members of the community again.

Big Two-Hearted Supermarket

KENT NUSSEY

Late in the afternoon, I walk over to the overpriced supermarket where I've been buying food for the past five years. At least every other day, I walk the several blocks to the big-city store and plod home burdened with two or three white plastic bags stuffed with groceries. Sometimes, walking thus, I think of days when I owned a car and the short magical drives I took through the fresh green countryside, the radio tuned to the oldies station, my spirit unexpectedly soaring when a particular song came on.

Back then, I lived in the basement of an empty house with a For Sale sign on the lawn; I was trying to finish a novel and laboured with a focus and faith that I assumed would sustain me forever. During the best hours of each day, I worked steadily in my well-insulated basement lair. In the summer, it was pleasantly dim and cool; in the winter, it was cozy and warm, a good place to write a novel, a good place to write anything. I honestly believed that all these hours, all this work, would ultimately propel me back into the world and reconnect me with all the good people and things I'd forfeited to finish my book. But when the doubts took hold, when a panic-stricken voice whispered in my ear while I prepared a meal or tried to read a newspaper, I'd jump into my car and drive out of town with the windows open and the radio playing. Whether it was the music or the detour through green fields and trees, I usually managed to touch the original sources of wonder in my life, if only for a few minutes. It was an absurdly simple and perhaps banal recipe for rejuvenation after hours at the typewriter (my father's old office-model Olympia electric, unwieldy as an out-board motor, with just as many moving parts) but it rarely failed to restore the connection. And not only did these skirmishes with wonder keep me writing, but they also sustained my belief in a greater world than the world of my book and the dark basement where I wrote it. Looking back, I recognize myself driving the country roads with a Dr. Pepper or an ice-cream sandwich in my hand, singing along to Roy Orbison or the Beach Boys, my mind bless-edly empty, my spirit running beside the car like the shadow that rippled over the blur of tall weeds and wildflowers, along the culverts and ditches and railroad crossings of the literal world that was so much bigger and realer than anything I could put in my book.

On this particular afternoon, I've come to the supermarket to escape the summer heat and smog as much as anything. On my way in, I notice that the tarps and scaffolding around the front have vanished. A new entranceway welcomes shoppers with wider doors and a vast banner that declares GRAND RE-OPENING, though the store never really closed. It's simply keeping pace with a neighbour-hood gone conspicuously upscale over the past three years. Wispy young film editors and compla-cent software designers now mingle over beets and lettuce heads with the ancient Italian men and swart Portuguese crones whose dark mutterings more or less express my own ambivalence about the changes.

It's peculiar how these trips, however necessary, have become a significant part of my daily routine. At this stage of my life, the routine is pretty much what I want it to be, and even if I'm a little thread-bare, I know that I've engineered my existence so that I can observe and process the various changes and, on good days, write about them. There are days, of course, when I can't write, when the bad air and heavy heat or the stereo from the first floor drive me from my desk, and I confess that lately these days have come too often. The creative fountainheads—the deep pools we ply with ex-asperation and cunning and nearly religious trepi-dation—seem to have gone dry. They still exist, I tell myself: I've just forgotten how to find them.

A few days earlier, I'd put the finishing touches on another novel. Like the first, the one written in the sparsely furnished basement, this book had con-sumed at least three years of my life. God knows why, but I often think of my first book when I'm grocery shopping. As I wander up and down the cold, clean aisles, I recollect hunching over the out-sized typewriter, the jammed space bar that forced me to hit the half-space twice between each word. I remember how the machine switched off with a hundred small clicks and whirs, and finally, a long rasping death rattle. I recall arriving at Grand Cen-tral Station with my manuscript wrapped in brown butcher paper in my knapsack, holding the knap-sack high like a trophy fish or duck beneath the gold clock while my friend snapped a photograph. Where's that picture now? Did I ever own a copy? I remember hiking across Manhattan in crisp fall weather, handing the book over to my agent in her office on the twenty-first floor.

The instant it left my hands I knew it would never be published. I knew I'd never recover the years of its making or the quantities of faith and clarity and passion that went into them.

We all know there's bad juju in such talk. Nobody asked me to be a writer. But surely there's limited harm in stating the obvious at this point in the game, and some good things came out of that first book. It earned me a life-saving grant, and I'd like to believe that the prolonged intensity of working on chapter after chapter made me a better writer. Of course, I'd made the dangerous mistake of thinking a single book could save me, but the years slowly disabused me of this belief without completely crushing my larger hope. I put the book in a drawer and retraced my steps to the cool, restorative waters of inspiration and motivation, of hope and ultimate wonder. Over time, these waters became harder to find, but if I looked, if I really sniffed and stared and trusted my instincts, I eventually stumbled onto the source.

With this second book—not just the several years of its composition, but the months of rewriting, the courting of agents and committing it to the mails—a new wooziness has washed over me, a sort of milky torpor compounded of emotional fatigue and genuine confusion. And though it ebbs and flows, changes shape and substance and tone, I can't seem to shake this ambivalence that keeps me from starting another novel. Every writer, probably every artist of any stripe, goes through stretches of inertia and ennui, and wisely refuses to discuss them. The malaise has different stages, distinct progressions that can be counterproductive or alarming without being terminal. The writing proceeds like the pulling of teeth or running uphill, with

blackouts and droughts and wrong-headed rushes across someone else's field. Remarking on these is acceptable, so long as it's clear that they're bits of bad luck and not fatal, because everyone knows that fatal cases exist, and if you contemplate their reality too long or too willingly, you might lose your poise and topple into the abyss.

Every writer has his own remedy for the malaise. If it's caught in the early stages, any number of psychological nostrums might work.

But with the completion and dispatch of this latest novel, an inescapable comparison to the first kicked in, and slowly I understood that if this book came back to me, if it came to rest atop the other one in the desk drawer, I might never write another. The publisher has yet to acknowledge receipt (and may not for weeks), but already the grimness has begun to sink in and I intuit that the conventional antidotes to literary disappointment—drink, travel, spending sprees—will prove useless or galling.

Years back, after I'd finished that first novel and decided a change of scenery might recharge the batteries, I drove with my friend Hopkins across the United States, from New York to California. My friend had a deadline on the coast, and we drove almost non-stop for three days and nights, travelling small country highways, napping under shade trees in public parks or cemeteries or dozing briefly in the car beside midnight cornfields. On the fourth morning, we pulled in at a sprawling new supermarket on the outskirts of San Jose. I recall coming in from the brutal heat, standing half-stunned in the overly air-conditioned aisles while Hopkins bought supplies, the road vibration draining from my numbed spine. Sleep-starved and disoriented, I beheld the order and clarity of the store with dawning awe. An even radiance came off the polished floors, the glossy fruits and vegetables. An otherworldly shine held the cans and the gleaming metal carts that rolled noiselessly around me. The old-style Muzak—those familiar instrumental versions of classic pop tunes—had a mentholated quality that matched the palpable contours of the place, its meaning in and out of time. I walked the maze of aisles in a sleep-deprived trance until a commotion at the checkout counters caught my attention. Two or three bag boys stared at something beyond the wide bank of windows that stretched between the entrance and exit. It took a moment to realize I was staring at fire, the orange waves sweeping the dry slopes around the parking lot. Through the spotless glass, we watched vivid flames leap on the near horizon, billows of milky smoke rising into the blue California sky. There were no alarms, no smell of smoke on the chill interior air, just the minty Muzak and the young mothers pushing their grocery-heaped carts and the interested commentary of the bag boys who kept working while they noted the advance of the flames outside.

I remember standing there: for a light-headed moment I didn't know where I was, perhaps even *who* I was. In one sense, a moment ripe with wonder; in another, an occasion of indefinite loss—the first time I felt, however dimly, some transparent but impenetrable obstruction come between my spirit and my capacity for wonder.

At that time, I had never doubted there were more books in me, more stories and essays and drawings. But that afternoon, for the first time in my life, I perceived the wonder of the world as something distinctly outside myself. Outside, but so near that I could have walked out into it, could have utterly immersed myself in it just by stepping through the automatic doors and strolling across the hot asphalt.

The present supermarket, mediated in part by the leathery oldsters yammering at each other in Mediterranean tongues, in part by the alien minor-key Muzak, lacks the dream-like intensity of the other. Yet each time I come here, some forgotten drawer or closet of memory opens, the senses drift, and the shadow of a powerful magic rises from the densely stacked shelves. The wavering shadow suggests nothing less than the possibility of the world, re-entry into wonder, and sometimes, when I touch a certain cooking spice or chrome utensil, I can almost imagine that world. But the shadow is only a shadow and I blank out, just as I did in California, with a spatula or syrup bottle in my hand, then blink awake when a small secret voice asks, "Will you ever write another book?"

Even in middle age, this is not a possibility I can readily process. It's not writer's block or fear of failure at work here, but in the course of my day, an average day spent unclogging a drain, paying the telephone bill, staring at a page, I might look up and squint, close my hand on thin air—and know that the deep wells of wonder and fascination have eluded me. The other afternoon I picked up a journal of mine from two years ago and marvelled at the excited voice in those pages crammed with quotations, observations, notes on the novel-in-progress. All this pictured a man splashing in the creative waters, drinking them from a cup engraved with stars and moons and dragons, a man who gasped happily as he fell backward into the deeps. Wonder fed the love of words; words created that hard edge of actuality; and all of it redeemed the absence of anything one might call a career. Swimming in the creative stuff, wading to my chin in it, I rarely doubted myself or my purpose.

Again, it's not fear of rejection or plain laziness (though God knows I'm lazy enough) I'm talking about here, but the loss of access to those creative deeps, the apprehension and delectation of the very texture of existence. You can read these qualities in

a thousand different kinds of sentences written by men and women who reached into the water and snatched them up into the daylight. A single sentence can shimmer with life's golden textures and seams for decades or centuries, long after the hand that wrote it has turned to grass. Such sentences, or a wisp of perfume on a city street, or an unexpected song in a moving car, can hold these golden textures. As a kid, in other supermarkets, I might hear the theme to the old *Route 66* TV show, or Vince Guaraldi playing "Cast Your Fate to the Wind," and I'd freeze in my tracks, possessed suddenly of a shivering high and the serene conviction that the world was made of miracles. Same as when, six or seven years ago, driving in my car, a song like "Wouldn't It Be Nice" came over the battered AM radio—that opening harp riff—and the road swerved up to heaven as sunshine filled my car. It sounds silly, I know, but it kept me going. If I apply my will and intelligence, I can remember the transcendence in the song, but I can't *feel* it as I once did, and I'm convinced that such a thing as mere feeling, rather than an idea or a plot, created the basis of faith that once prompted me to undertake a writing project that might take two or three years to finish. That faith, the unspoken conviction that I'd feel this way forever . . . losing this, I maintain, is not the symptom of any of the myriad adult neuroses that writers limp along with or brush away like flies. It's more like losing a prized volume from your library: the book is not missed at first, but one day, someone mentions Shakespeare and you think, "Say, I haven't read *The Tempest* in a long time—" and when you reach for your *Collected Plays*, the handsome edition you've owned since college, it's gone. Who did you lend it to? When did it go out of your house?

But it's no use. The book, as familiar and reassuring as your father's watch, has vanished.

The supermarket Muzak makes me irritable. The songs all sound alike, sung robotically by the skinny clones of one skinny girl who lives in a mansion in London or L.A., or by nasty adenoidal boys who never owned a dog or threw a stone at a crow. Or maybe these songs are fine, completely adequate, only I can't hear them for being too long separated from the magic waters, for being too far out on a limb and self-involved.

I open the heavy glass door, drop a tray of frozen Swedish meatballs into my plastic basket, and move on.

A few feet ahead, in the soft-drink section, a tall blonde woman in a maroon business suit fires clipped questions into the tiny cell phone pressed to her hair. As she struggles with a six-pack of Diet Pepsi, the gesture reveals a physicality, a *humanness* that strikes me as poignant in contrast to her words. She's buying, selling, doing what people do in the world. I've encountered her multi-tasking species at parties, in bars, and always, after an initial exchange between us that establishes our common hipness and class, comes the moment when I explain what I do, or try to do, with my time. And the next moment, when my nerve falters and I blurt involuntarily: "I live like a graduate student, I haven't owned a car for years! To tell the truth, I've no idea how I've gotten this far!" And she, a single mother who manages a chain of fitness centres or

gardening stores, pushes a frosted strand of hair from her tired but handsome face and congratulates me and declares that I must never look back or down, then excuses herself to make a call. And as she vanishes into the crowd, I realize that I have disappointed her, that in appearance and diction and demeanour I seemed to be her exact social counterpart. But the truth comes out inevitably, and it's the transparency of my shame, I suppose, rather than the facts I've revealed that causes her to turn away.

This one glances in my direction with a wan smile and shifts her grocery cart so that I may pass, the phone still glued to her hair.

In the aisle of household wares, Hopkins comes to mind. When we met, in San Francisco in the 1980s, we both entertained hopes and notions that went with a broader conception of what it meant to be a writer—specifically, a writer of novels. Hopkins came from an old and wealthy San Francisco family, but he had educated himself in the rough-and-tumble American Romantic tradition, graduating from prep schools to jobs that involved hard travel and manual labour. After one year at Princeton, he dropped out to work on the railroad. For one whole Nebraskan winter, he lived in an old caboose with seven other guys as they worked slowly up the line. In the spring, he hitchhiked to Oregon and drove a truck for a logging outfit until he ruined his knee on the job and drifted back to the Bay Area with seven hundred pages of an unfinished novel in his duffle bag. Square-jawed and rangy, with piercing blue eyes and black sideburns, he seemed like a hybrid of Doc Holliday and Jack Kerouac, a western adventurer with poetry in his veins. He could quote from Milton, the Bible, and *Moby Dick*. He'd known dangerous characters, could lift his shirt and show you peculiar scars. For weeks after entering the writing workshop at Stanford, he slept in his car, even though his family's home was no more than an hour from the campus.

That first year I knew him, both Hopkins and I had girlfriends who wrote short stories. I loved and practised the story form myself, but over cheap beers in dingy waterfront taverns, Hop and I agreed that the novel was a writer's true proving ground, a genre still capable of making waves in the world. We confessed our ambitions, recited scenes and characters we loved from the classics, and from our own lives, recounted episodes we planned to con-

vert into immutable fiction. That fond writerly caveat was always in the air: "This is my story, you can't have it, but let me tell you about a guy I knew in Omaha—" or a car accident in Vancouver, or the Playboy Club in Des Moines. It was all grist for the mill, and the mill functioned admirably and eagerly then.

That fall, to our shared surprise, Hop's girlfriend won a berth in the *Best American Short Stories* collection. Raymond Carver had judged the work; in the book's introduction, he had declared that she was on the brink of a brilliant career. The four of us celebrated her success with a weekend at a cabin up in Point Reyes. Hop and I contributed two magnums of good champagne; the women brought steaks and seafood and two bags of the strongest, richest coffee I'd ever tasted. For three days we carried on, drinking champagne with sirloins or clams, getting high at midnight and dancing, asking Hop's girlfriend how it felt to be famous. The last morning, he and I found an old BB gun beneath the elevated back porch. We strung an enormous onion head from a tree seven or eight yards beyond the porch and took turns shooting at it. The gun fired a slow, arcing BB you could follow with your eye. We devised an elaborate contest with the swaying head, the off-true gun, and the huge half-full bottle of champagne. We drank and shot at the onion while the women sat and smoked behind us, redigesting all the details of the literary coup. That night, back in my girlfriend's apartment in Palo Alto, she burst into anguished tears and swore that one day she too would appear in *Best American Short Stories*. If she accomplished nothing else, this she would do. And some fifteen years later, long after we'd parted, a story of hers appeared in that collection and I wondered what it meant to her that late in the game. Did it feel as good as being young and drinking champagne and making love in a strange bed?

Perhaps there is no "late" or "game." I suppose that I, for one, should hope this is true.

Several years after my ex-girlfriend's appearance in the *Best American* anthology, she resurfaced again. This time with an essay in *Granta* about her own struggles with the writing life, particularly delineating the stresses of having a literary celebrity for a partner, for now she was living with a man who had written a wildly successful novel, a man who had won real fame and the secular validation she had so wholeheartedly yearned for all these years.

After reading the piece, I recollected our youthful excesses and minor triumphs, the intimacies and tears, our mutual vows to keep the faith, and I wondered if our interpretations—hers and mine—of that faith had been fundamentally different from the start. I wondered if we had ever meant the same thing when we talked about writing and publishing, about what distinguished books from literature and writers from artists. I wonder if any two people can mean the same thing when they discuss such matters.

In any event, I eventually drifted back east, and Hopkins and the mammoth novel he carried in his bag were never heard of again. Both our girlfriends had their public successes, moments when everything seemed possible, moments whose sweetness lay in the implicit promise that life was just starting,

that this success was only the first in a string of ever brighter, braver ones. Perhaps Hopkins and I had our own moments, too, when we gazed on the solidity of our manuscripts, hefted the undeniable weight of them in our hands. A different sort of moment, to be sure, and the meaning of that solidity has changed with time, but even in the obscure darkness of my desk drawer those pages will occasionally sing to me. Softly, a little sadly, they sing "I Will Wait for You" or "Cast Your Fate to the Wind." Standing in this supermarket aisle of cheap drinking glasses and aluminum foil—a pool of emptiness in an otherwise busy store—I hear the ghostly music sift down the years; I consider all the unpublished manuscripts, however fragmented or substantial, never to be known in the world—the ones that sleep in suitcases or under beds, that sing softly of the young men and women who made them out of hunger and hope, the best parts of their youth; the young men and women who have become the battle-scarred adults who now commit their practised and marketable thoughts to thin disks that might slip out of a breast pocket when they stoop to tie their shoes. My generation, in its youth, was probably the last to write their first novels and stories on paper, on typewriters with hard moving parts that made a masculine clatter. We, at least, have those dense and weighty blocks of paper we can lift with two hands and, at the very least, gather some vague architectural sense of what our time and talent disappeared into.

A commotion behind me: a chunky kid complains to his mother—it might be his grandmother—that he's bored, that he wants to go home. The matriarch, swart, squat, and oblivious, grumbles an imperative and pushes her cart along.

I follow them toward the deli section near the entrance, turn left, and there, three feet in front of me, I see something that doesn't quite register, that takes me moments to recognize.

Before me, in this endlessly rejuvenated and reorganized store, an enormous glass tank of living fish stands atop the seafood cooler that displays the iced flesh of their dead cousins. I move closer. They're trout, smallish rainbows, finning dazedly, half-stunned, staring out at me exactly as I stare in at them. I move still closer and press a fingertip to the inch of glass that separates their small gaping faces from my hand.

And then there is using everything.

Gertrude Stein

It's like staring at the problem that I haven't even been able to conceptualize as a problem. The answer's behind the problem, and the problem is just behind this glass, staring back at me. I can see it, but I can't get my mind around how it works, how it has been pressing me down for so long.

It's something I read that felt inseparable from something I did; it's in a burned-out landscape, or the burned-out landscape as imagined by a man on the brink of a change he cannot even contemplate. It's the conversation between the man and the boy who fishes a different river, not even a river but a deep pool in a tributary to the river. He rode his bike down the two-lane highway and followed the tractor path through the cornfield a hundred yards to this hole. He sits, legs dangling, on a rough-hewn timber bridge no bigger than a raft. The bridge makes a cool shadow on the deep green pool. An occasional truck blats by in the near distance, but the rest is silence and the creaky whistle of blackbirds in the stand of sumacs between him and the field. Now and then, the cheap fibreglass pole twitches and he pulls up a fat mud-pout or catfish. Hardly big game, but tricky to hook. The serene focus that went into the catching of those sorry fish was unlike anything that had come since, unless he compared it to the absorption he lavished on his typewriter in the early days, so lost in the page that he allowed the moving carriage to knock the mug of hot coffee he'd absently set too near the machine. But no, that was different. That seemed like the making of wonder, but actually it was the tapping of it. He seemed to be catching fish, but really he was emptying the pond.

One day he rode his bike home with three bullheads on the stringer dangling from his handlebar. When he parked the bike in his yard, a skinny stray cat came mewling from the shadows and nearly climbed his leg to get at the fish. He dropped one before the skin-and-bones cat and in minutes it was devoured without a trace—not a fin or spine, not a smear in the grass. He tossed another and again the cat quickly crunched it down, masticating the thorny fish head with a hunger that bordered on miraculous.

Hunger. Real hunger. Something he didn't know then.

And solitude. He didn't understand it then, but he hungered after solitude when he rode along to the fishing hole below the country highway. You can't work those pools without loving the silence.

But far down the years, you find yourself staring at a tank full of traumatized trout and you see something else that got between you and the water. Disappointment. Even worse, unacknowledged disappointment—the kind that trips you up in the most ho-hum transactions of an average day. The kind that costs you intimacy and love and the brilliance of the morning. You ask, How did that get in there? Yet it's so obvious. It has so obviously been riding with you for years and years.

Did you know what you were doing when you covered yourself with solitude and worked so single-mindedly without counting the years? Or were you just angling on the void, pushing ever deeper into a vast and seductive dreaminess even as you emptied the pond?

My heart tightens as I stare at the hovering trout. For an instant, I feel that close to the form-

less question; for the sheerest instant I feel all the old feeling.

It was a long time since Nick had looked into a stream and seen trout.

I turn away from the tank and push through the crowd until I find the canned goods. Scanning the shelves, I grab a can of spaghetti, then pork and beans. At home I'll stir both into a skillet, scoop it hot onto my plate and eat it all.

Nick was hungry. He did not believe he had ever been hungrier . . . "Chrise," Nick said, "Geezus Chrise," he said happily.

At my age, one never knows where such experiments can lead. If hunger is still hunger, anything is possible. And there will be coffee, the way I remember it. Coffee according to Hopkins. Already I see the lid coming up, the grounds running down the side of the pot.

It will make a good ending to the story.

Two Poems

W. S. MERWIN

To That Stretch of Canal

Spring is here dearie I seen a robin
up the canal this morning froze to death
                                    — Canal neighbour

By now the towpath leads on without you
who were the only reason it was there
in the days that went on barges when you
were young and they vanished on the long sky where
you carried them and when I first saw you
nothing was left of them except that sky
in your later life when I would know you
on summer evenings watching swallows fly
low to your surface and when ice held you
all winter though you were slipping away
even then and what now remains of you
but this long dry grave a shallow valley
and shreds of marsh in the last tracks of you
with things still waving that were thrown away

To Billy's Car

You were not going anywhere

any more

with your nose to the wall
and your cracked tires
but it seems you went just the same
and nobody noticed

by then we ourselves had gone
from the smell of your mildewed velvets
and the mica hue of the world
through your windows after supper
and the touch of your numb controls

by then the model airplanes
I suppose were no longer turning
on their strings under the ceiling
of the silent room kept
the way Billy's dead brother had left it
and his grandmother had stopped
baking cakes and crying
at all the dying
she kept mumbling over

and by that time no doubt
the girl we talked about
with whom we were both in love
who went to a different school
so that we never saw her
except in the choir on Sunday
had married somebody else
with a lot of money

looking through your old windshield
that had been there all winter
we could see the grass
that was growing on the wall that year
as we went on talking
into the spring evening

Snake-Eating

JIM HARRISON

Everyone knows that if Adam and Eve had eaten the snake rather than the apple, the world would be a better place, but then, intelligent Canadians will query, better than what? The parallel world bandied about by the ancients where our land is sea, and our sea land? Jealous Christian men are forever worried that small dogs, male cats, and snakes are looking up their wives' skirts, forgetting the hundreds of species of insects that have vivid sexual lives. They have also forgotten the message of the Gnostic Gospels that as members of the mammalian species, we must eat our fears. When my old English setter Tess was startled during her nap in the yard by an emerging gopher, she quickly killed and ate this Republican beast who undermines the foundation of our existence, the ground.

The girl drove into the countryside on a warm August morning turning into the driveway of an abandoned farmstead feeling edgy because for the first time she was steering a car in her night clothes and without panties.

This is a complicated essay that demands a little sexual content to keep the attention of the readers, especially the millions of distraught hockey fans who now drink beer while staring into broom closets. On a recent trip to Toronto, a prominent Canadian critic, who doesn't wish to be outed on the matter, quipped that the novels of Updike, Roth, and DeLillo could be much improved if skin pictures were interspersed in the pages. He was drinking a large glass of anisette without ice and I let the suggestion, obviously a good idea, pass without comment. I'm not going to go out on a limb that has no tree attached. Everyone knows that modern criticism is a gated community and that the literary ethos of our time is contraction, an etiolated minimalism where the corpse is sat on to expel the last breath of living air.

Back to snakes. The first rattlesnake I ate was cooked by a retired surgeon at streamside while we were taking a lunch break during trout fishing. We were in a canyon in Montana where the crotalids abounded. I thought my surgeon friend did a rather clumsy job of skinning the snake and said so, at which point he admitted his surgeon's degree had come mail order from Phoenix, Arizona. Sure, he had lost a lot of patients, but he and his family had had a nice life and that's what's important in California. When he flopped the whole rattler on the hot coals it contracted in an alarming imitation of life, with the snake's departing soul seeming to hang there in the rancid smoke. The meat was fairly good with a lot of salt, pepper, and Tabasco, reminding me of the muskrat of my youth that we ate on our little farm near the Big Swamp in northern Michigan.

She deftly shed her blue peignoir and climbed the apple tree with the grace of a gibbon.

Bite after bite we chew our food with the kind of quiet heroism that is unacknowledged by sporting journalists. In a culture in a state of severe decay, the peripheral always subsumes the primary; thus my exploits as a bold eater and mountain climber have been given short shrift in a world of skating and pucks. How proud I was on that zero-degree morning that I gave up being a hockey goalie for the warm, albeit musty, halls of the arts, and for scaling peaks unknown to others in the mountain-climbing fraternity. True mountains are not to be measured in numbers, any more than saying that a beautiful girl is five feet eight inches tall describes her qualitative aspects, say the back of her knees, which are as soft as a mole's tummy.

Life seems to be taking my breath away. Last year at age sixty-six, I climbed a nineteen-thousand-foot mountain in Mexico called Orizaba and still had to do the cooking at base camp at eleven thousand feet because other members of the expedition were the typical fruit-and-granola ninnies. Naturally at this height soufflés are out of the question. I made a stew of a smallish but overripe boa constrictor with haberno peppers and squash. This snake tastes a bit like the chow dog I had been served and had unwittingly eaten in northern Mongolia. I admit that the boa constrictor put me off snake eating in the year that followed, though there were definite aphrodisiac qualities. I made love to three Mexican women after we danced to internal music on a ledge with a mile-high drop. At dawn I cooked us a middling omelette from the eggs of the local monkey-eating eagle, averting my eyes from the pink embryos, which are improbably nutritious. I had to carry Michael (he pronounces it Michel), the expedition poet, down the mountain because he had stubbed his toe on a book he had been forbidden to carry. We all know certain dweebs who can't go to the toilet or make love without a book or laptop in their company. Halfway to Veracruz, we had to wait three hours at a thatched-roof restaurant for our tacos while a twelve-year-old girl poached what I thought was a boa's head but turned out to be a beef tongue. Like fish, snakes are better cooked fresh and no refrigeration was available, while well-salted beef tongue can last for weeks even on the equator. While I slept in the dirt with the dogs, Michael tried to seduce the girl. She stabbed him in his stubbed toe with an ice pick, which stymied his sexual impulses. When we reached Veracruz, I swam a few miles out in the harbour to inspect the propeller of the Greek freighter, pushing away at the last possible moment when the vindictive captain started the twelve-thousand-horsepower engine and put the ship in gear. When I swam back to the Emporio, I thought of owning twelve thousand horses, but then, my Montana ranchette is only ten acres.

This year my breath is too short to make the Orizaba climb. We killed seventy-three rattlers last summer on my Montana property, but I haven't the gusto to eat the few that I saved in the freezer. It's a little like a teenager who gets drunk on gin, pukes, and then is intolerant of this liquor, and may very well puke again while showering with juniper or pine-scented soap. Our fragile minds fill up with taboos as our lives pass. A Venezuelan Indian tribe, no matter how close to starvation, will not eat an anaconda that has devoured one of their children.

Curiously, our godlike intelligences, rarely used, can differentiate between similar species. Who can resist a hot bowl of anguillas, "baby eels," in their bath of olive oil and garlic? If we didn't eat these babies, they would end up swimming as many as seven thousand miles to the Sargasso Sea to mate before returning to their homeland estuarine waters. Try to imagine, if you will, spending your entire life underwater.

The girl hung by her knees from an apple tree limb giving a blue jay a peculiar view of her parts. The bird shrieked in alarm.

Perhaps the very last snake I will ever eat was during the Athens Olympics last summer. I had stupidly gotten involved with an ex-ballerina in New York City who had become a performance artist, a category of the arts that I find difficult to hold clearly in mind. It was a pathetic case of geezer lust and my little sack of Viagras were crumbling in the humidity so that I dried the damp blue powder with her hair dryer and snorted it like cocaine in the days of yore. I also had undiagnosed diabetes, so I was either asleep or furious and missed the prime event, women's synchronized swimming. I was dozing in a nightclub when my ditzy performance artist was doing her food-chain routine by trying to throw spaghetti marinara to a litter of unweaned piglets. No one from New York knows, but certainly country folk are aware that unweaned piglets are interested in only mother's milk. The crowd booed, she was inconsolable and ran out the back door into the Athens night. The nightclub owner, a faux Zorba type, wanted to cook one of the piglets. I find false heartiness repellent and wandered over to the Thai compound to see a friend and there was served a viper stew, the snake supposedly killed fresh that morning in the mountains of Thessalonika. Food is as much a crapshoot as literature, and I wondered later if venom in the stew had entered a wound where I bit my lip after ingesting too much Viagra.

Where we winter in Patagonia, Arizona, is the only area in the United States with seven types of rattlesnakes, but I'm no longer tempted. The javelinas that eat the snakes are much more interesting on the plate, though when butchering a javelina you must be careful to carve out the rank scent glands, which are reminiscent of a Republican wife after an inaugural ball. On warm moonlit evenings, we watch the rattlers do their horizontal dances in the yard.

The girl dropped from the apple tree and ran through the orchard grass so loose-limbed that she was kicking her own pale butt.

Tomorrow I have to endure a medical procedure in Tucson that involves a twenty-four hour fast. This is new territory for me and I suspect that I'll feel not a little like my old hero Gandhi. With-

out being unpleasantly specific, I will reveal that the surgeon, who apparently has a valid licence, will visit my innards from two directions to discover which of my fifteen-thousand meals caused the cherry bomb explosion a few weeks ago. Take it from me, seven jalapenos is one too many in a Thai pork dish. Sometimes I wonder if my wisdom is in decline. When I hear the expression "the wisdom of the body," I am puzzled. Perhaps I have eaten too much of the world? An elephant's anus cooked in a hole of hot rocks by the Kikuyu in Africa could have done the wrong job, or was it the thousand-year-old sea cucumber in Shanghai? Maybe it was mom's super-dry pot roast or Labrador's fermented caribou. My DNA has troubled Tucson medical authorities to the extent that Menninger's had been suggested rather than Mayo. Last winter in the Yucatan, a very old legless Mayan chieftain asked me seriously if I was part dog after his vicious guard dogs tried to climb on my lap in instant friendship. I wonder. Maybe it's time to be someone else? After a month of eating mostly yogourt and rice, I have dreamt that I'm camping on a glacier as white as my food. O, how I crave a braised pork jowl swimming in its fat, a Szechuan chicken cooked in a couple pounds of bird peppers, or even a simple white truffle the size of a baseball grated on a bowl of pasta.

Back in the car she sat nudely on the hot mammalian leather of the seat.

R. du Croissant, 16.   Chez Aubert, Pl. de la Bourse, 29.   Imp. d'Aubert &

Grrrrande hostilités!!! Les éditeurs du *Brîque* font leurs décisions pour le nouvelle édition.

ROBERT CREELEY

Some Remembrances

I am just one of the hundreds of poets Robert Creeley personally knew and personally touched, and just one of thousands who were not poets, who took his poems in whole and deep. Within minutes of the fabulous Creeleys' move to Providence I was going around saying, *Dig it.* I wondered if he stayed in my earshot much longer he would not go around saying, *Goddammit.* But he wasn't profane, never anything but supremely gentle and graceful. He said lucid, significant things. He laughed readily. He quoted as if it were breathing—defining statements, words to live by—and the source could be a ballad, a relative, Pound, Olson, or literally, a passerby whose scrap of conversation he tuned in to. He absorbed the wisdom commonly available to humans and so aggressively ignored by most. He could instantly identify valuable information and give it shape and his very particular breath. He was a monologist who had become the ideally responsive listener. He was a compact, intense, and all but omnipresent maker of poems, whose command of a room was absolute, whether he sat quietly in the background of the kitchen's hubbub, hands folded across his lap, or appeared in a crowded hall as if out of a cloud. The rivet in his direction was involuntary. If you wanted his approval you needn't go begging, for not only did he never withhold it, he volunteered it. He made his poetry livable, durable. He included us. You wanted to lean into him like a barn. Or draw your chair near his fire. You wanted to take his hand so everyone would see and would know, *This is my friend.* If Bob could make poetry his life, and he did, the rest of us doubters can be assured that poetry really matters. Oh man, we have to make good on what he gave us. We have to aim true to make our language bear up to his light.

— C. D. Wright

. . . all that industrious wis-

dom lives in the way the mountains
and the desert are waiting
for the heroes, and death also
can still propose the old labors.

— Robert Creeley, "Heroes"

Fabulous tales of drunken nights and big fights— these were the first stories I heard about Robert Creeley, told by Bobbie Louise Hawkins (once Bobbie Creeley) when I was a student at Naropa in the late eighties/early nineties. One of the tastiest morsels: ". . . so, I turned around and punched Bob in his good eye. . . ." Young poets thrive on such tales of poetry's heroes, especially when told by those who knew and loved those heroes from up close. I don't remember the first time I met Bob Creeley, but I do remember being surprised again and again by his generosity and thoughtfulness—his attention to the world and humans, his willingness to connect. Sharp-eyed. The last time I saw him Laird Hunt (my husband) and I were driving him from Boulder to Denver this past October. He wanted to take the scenic route, though he seemed to pay no attention to what was going on outside the car. I was driving, Bob was in the passenger seat, his good eye was window-side. He seemed as energetic as ever; he had the physical wealth of a man in his thirties. We were talking about his switch from New Directions to the University of California Press. I asked if University of California would do his new books as well as his reprints. He turned his face fully toward me, so his good eye could take me in (much, I imagined, as does the driving speaker in "I Know a Man"). "I don't have more than a book or two left," he said, in that completely candid way he had that made things seem grim and tender and funny all at once. "I'm old, don't you know." Seventy-eight applied to him as a kind of loose-fitting number, but "old" didn't, just in the way that his poems will never seem old. In Denver (where Bob requested a simple place for dinner), we wound up at a Middle Eastern restaurant where a belly dancer with a sword between her teeth kept eyeing Bob, but that is another story.

— Eleni Sikelianos

This great poet, Robert Creeley, 1926–2005:

Room for one and all
around the gathering ball,
to hold the sacred thread,
to hold and wind and pull.

— Robert Creeley, "The Ball"
During a recent visit, laughing, we imaged ourselves as the last of the Mohicans. His is the "recognition of things through the act of writing itself"—"It was poetry that got us here, and now we have to go too." Intimate "what" and "ever" exactly.

— Robin Blaser

I was in Rochester in the sixties, in the winter, and there was a terrible snowstorm. I was there to give a reading, and in the middle of it, I saw Robert and Bobbie come in and sit down, and it turned out they'd come to drive me back to Buffalo in the snowstorm. Afterward, when we left, there was almost no one on the road—fortunately, as otherwise I would probably not be here tonight.

As we drove along, Creeley was talking and driving the car, and waving his hands. He had only one eye and his hands were flying around as he talked, and Bobbie was talking, and I was trying to get a word in edgewise. And one of Robert's hands hit the dashboard and all the lights in the car went out. We could see the snowstorm through the windshield, and I had to presume we were still on the road because we had not driven off the edge or hit anything, and all of us were still talking, with the snowflakes giving almost enough light to see by, and Creeley somehow keeping the car on the road. After a minute or so, Bobbie reached under the dash and flipped something and the lights came back on. A complete moment, and wonderful thing to remember a friend, and another poet, by.

— W. S. Merwin

Bresson's Movies

A movie of Robert
Bresson's showed a yacht,
at evening on the Seine,
all its lights on, watched

by two young, seemingly
poor people, on a bridge adjacent,
the classic boy and girl
of the story, any one

one cares to tell. So
years pass, of course, but
I identified with the young,
embittered Frenchman,

knew his almost complacent
anguish and the distance
he felt from his girl.
Yet another film

of Bresson's has the
aging Lancelot with his
awkward armor standing
in a woods, of small trees,

dazed, bleeding, both he
and his horse are,
trying to get back to
the castle, itself of

no great size. It
moved me, that
life was after all
like that. You are

in love. You stand
in the woods, with
a horse, bleeding.
The story is true.

— Robert Creeley

A Message from the Publisher

Any issue of a literary magazine is momentous, given that it manages to appear in a world obsessed with body counts and scandalous nipples, but this particular issue of *Brick* is *especially* special. It is our seventy-fifth (in a row!), and to celebrate, we're breaking out the king cans and throwing a party. Not like that party we had for our twenty-fifth anniversary—an evening nobody remembers in much detail—but a virtual party, in the pages of this very issue. For herein lies more than your average *Brick*, the delights of which you know only too well.

Brick 75 isn't just great between the covers, though. You'll note our unusual packaging this time, due to the presence of a mini-*Brick*, which is, in fact, a catalogue. It contains images of manuscript pages that were created by some of our favourite writers expressly for *Brick*'s seventy-fifth issue. You'll find in it the handiwork of Alice Munro, Don DeLillo, Michael Ondaatje, Pico Iyer, Margaret Atwood, Sharon Olds, Jim Harrison, Michael Chabon, Marilynne Robinson, Julian Barnes, Jonathan Lethem, A. L. Kennedy and many more. And the really fun part is this: you could own any or all of these manuscript pages. Because beginning on June 16, 2005, shortly after the appearance of this issue of *Brick*, each original manuscript page will be auctioned off on eBay. You will be able to link to the auctions from our website (www.brick mag.com) or you can find them at eBay.com by searching for the keywords *Brick* and *fundraiser* as well as the last name of the author whose work you're interested in. These rarities will go to the highest bidders, and the money raised will be used to keep *Brick* in ink and stamps. Keep us going for another twenty-five issues, and perhaps we'll throw a real party again.

On another front, our fondest congratulations to Michael Henry of Robert's Creek, B.C., who won a ten-year Sponsor Subscription by being one of 150 loyal subscribers to respond to a readers' survey we included with all our Canadian mailings last fall. Guided by the insightful responses to our questions (some of which were downright nosey), we'll be able to chart a truer course in the future. But just because you're not a Canadian subscriber doesn't mean you can't tell us what you love or love-slightly-less about *Brick*. We're always interested in what you're thinking. E-mail your questions, grievances, marriage proposals, botanical insights and so on to info@brickmag.com.

Thank you for joining us on this big anniversary. We hope we're making the phrase "thick as a brick" a positive one in your home.

— *Michael Redhill*

The Usual Suspects

Milton Acorn, "the People's Poet," was born in Charlottetown, P.E.I., in 1923. He spent his life writing and working in Montreal, Toronto, and Vancouver, although he died at his birthplace, in 1986. He was the author of fifteen books of poetry, among them *Jawbreakers* and *I've Tasted My Blood*. In 1975, Acorn was given the Governor General's Award for Poetry for *The Island Means Minago*.

Martin Berkovitz is a painter, draftsman, and print-maker. His work has been exhibited in Toronto, at the Pollock Gallery, the Moos Gallery (no relation), and Gallery One, as well as in the United States and Europe. He lives in New Mexico.

Alastair Bland, a twenty-six-year-old San Francisco native, is a frequent contributor to publications such as the *San Francisco Bay Guardian*, the British quarterly *Petits Propos Culinaires*, and the food website Egullet.com. His writing often details his travels, from living off the land in Baja, California to his two-thousand-mile "sustainable living" bike trip. Bland has a degree in anthropology and geology from U.C. Santa Barbara.

Roo Borson's *Short Journey Upriver Toward Oishida* was published by McClelland & Stewart in 2004 and won the Governor General's Award. With Kim Maltman and Andy Patton, Borson is a member of the collaborative writing group Pain Not Bread, whose *Introduction to the Introduction to Wang Wei* was published in 2000 by Brick Books.

Born in England, **Rosalind Brackenbury** now lives in Key West, Florida. Her latest novel is *The House in Morocco*, published by Toby Press in 2003, and she has just finished the novel *The Third Swimmer*.

Amit Chaudhuri has written four novels (the most recent of which is *A New World*), a book of short stories, and an acclaimed critical study of D. H. Lawrence's poetry. Chaudhuri has won several awards, including the Los Angeles Times Book Prize and the Indian government's highest literary honour, the Sahitya Akademi Award.

Kevin Connolly was one of the founding editors of *what*, the seminal magazine of arts and criticism that ran between 1984 and 1990. He has published three collections of poetry, the most recent of which, *drift*, has just been released by House of Anansi Press.

In March 2004, **Brad Cran** was awarded the inaugural Vancouver Arts Award commission in writing and publishing. He is currently at work on the book-length version of *Cinéma Vérité*.

Rackstraw Downes's work can be found in the Art Institute of Chicago, the Metropolitan Museum of Art, the Museum of Modern Art, and the Whitney Museum of American Art. In 1999 he was inducted into the American Academy and Institute of Arts and Letters. He lives in New York.

Michael Elcock lives on Vancouver Island with his wife Marilyn Bowering. His non-fiction book *A Perfectly Beautiful Place* has recently been published by Oolichan Books, and is distributed by the University of Toronto Press.

Carolyn Forché's most recent book, *Blue Hour* (HarperCollins, 2003), was a finalist for the Na-

tional Book Critics Circle Award. She teaches at Skidmore College in Saratoga Springs, N.Y.

Jim Harrison's new collection of novellas, *The Summer He Didn't Die*, will be released in August 2005 by Grove/Atlantic.

Michael Helm was born in the wilds of Saskatchewan. He is now an editor at *Brick*. His novels are *The Projectionist* and *In the Place of Last Things*.

Abbey Huggan is a part-time mature student in printmaking, bookbinding, and papermaking at the Ontario College of Art and Design in Toronto.

Apart from mounting art exhibitions, **Av Isaacs** published books and records of contemporary music and sponsored poetry readings, underground film screenings, mixed media concerts, and happenings. Over a period of close to fifty years, the Isaacs Gallery was a driving force of the Toronto art scene.

Pico Iyer, currently lost somewhere in the Himalayas, is the author, most recently, of *Sun after Dark*, a book of travels to the poorest corners of the world, and a novel, *Abandon*, which bears no relation at all to the work of John Fowles.

Nadine McInnis is the author of three books of poetry; a book of literary criticism; and a collection of short stories, *Quicksilver*, published by Raincoast Books in 2001. She has recently completed the poetry manuscript *Two Hemispheres*, which includes the essay that appears in this issue. Her bilingual collection of new and selected poems, *First Fire / Ce feu qui dévore*, will appear in 2005.

W. S. Merwin, in over fifty years of writing, has published almost thirty books of original poetry, as well as works in translation. This year will see the publication of a new collection entitled *Migration: Selected Poems 1951-2001*, in addition to *Present Company*, a book of new poems. Both books will be published by Copper Canyon Press.

Leilah Nadir is an Iraqi-Canadian living in Vancouver, British Columbia. She has written a play, *Heavenly Bodies*; a collection of short stories, *Bazaar*; and a novel, *Still*. Since the invasion of Iraq, she has been a commentator on that country for the CBC, the *Globe and Mail*, and the *Georgia Straight*.

Kent Nussey is the author of *The War in Heaven* and is a frequent contributor to *Brick*. His most recent book is the novel *A Love Supreme*. He lives in Toronto.

Don Paterson, Scottish poet and musician, won the 2004 T. S. Eliot Award for *Landing Light*. He is poetry editor at Picador and teaches at the University of St. Andrews. He is the author, most recently, of *The Book of Shadows*, a collection of aphorisms.

Vasco Ray has lived with the BaAka for twenty years, recording their music and writing about them. There are many books on the BaAka and other pygmy groups in central Africa, and numer-

ous recordings of their music. Two publications that combine text, photos, and music recordings are *Seize the Dance!* by Michelle Kisliuk and *Bayaka* by Louis Sarno.

Donald Richie, ex-curator of film at the New York Museum of Modern Art, is best known as the leading Western authority on Japanese film, but he has also written on many other aspects of the country in books such as *The Inland Sea* and the collection released in 2001 as *The Donald Richie Reader*. During his more than fifty years residence in Japan, Richie kept a detailed record of his life there, which has been collected in his book *The Japan Journals*.

Dominic Sansoni has worked as a photographer in Sri Lanka since 1980. He has just completed work on a book on Sri Lankan architecture and interiors, and will next finish work on a small book on colour in Sri Lanka. What he likes doing best is travelling in Asia with no agenda.

Norman Mailer has called **Michael Silverblatt** "the best reader in America." As host of KCRW's *Bookworm*, a show he created in 1989 for the station, Silverblatt has interviewed more than a thousand authors, covering the entire landscape of arts and letters. He lives in Santa Monica, California.

Susan Sontag, the American writer and critic, was the author of seventeen books, including *Against Interpretation* and *The Volcano Lover*. Sontag's novel *In America* won the American National Book

Award in 2000. She died in December of 2004, at the age of seventy-one.

Chris Ware is the author of *Jimmy Corrigan: The Smartest Kid on Earth*, which received the Guardian First Book Award in 2001 and was also included in the 2002 Whitney Biennial. He recently edited the thirteenth issue of *McSweeney's Quarterly Concern*, and a collection of his dismissable humorous material, *The ACME Novelty Library*, will be released in the fall.

Lawrence Weschler was a staff writer at *The New Yorker* for twenty years and is now the director of the New York Institute for the Humanities at NYU, where he has founded the magazine *Omnivore*. His most recent book, *Vermeer in Bosnia*, came out with Pantheon Books last year, and this fall McSweeney's Publishing will release his new work, *Everything That Rises: A Book of Convergences*.

Christopher Zinn is the executive director of the Oregon Council for the Humanities. He has taught at Reed College, and lectures and writes frequently about American literature and culture.

Credits

The quote on our spine comes from C. D. Wright's re-membrance of Robert Creeley on page 163 of this issue of *Brick*.

page 2, 17, 22, 26, 27, 62, 72, 112, 123, 135, 152, 161: Courtesy of Valance Archives.

page 5, after page 96: These drawings, by Chris Ware, will appear in *The ACME Novelty Datebook, Volume 2*, available in 2006 from Drawn and Quarterly Books.

page 7: Excerpt from "Camus' *Notebooks*" from *Against Interpretation* by Susan Sontag. Copyright © 1964, 1966, renewed 1994 by Susan Sontag. Reprinted by permission of Farrar, Straus and Giroux, LLC.

page 9: Painting by David Hockney; photo of painting by Richard Schmidt. Courtesy of the Richard Gray Gallery.

page 10: Painting by Breyten Breytenbach. Courtesy of Lawrence Weschler.

page 11: From the Torqued Ellipses exhibition by Richard Serra. Photo by Dirk Relnartz, courtesy of the Museum of Contemporary Art in Los Angeles.

page 13, 84, 89, 92: Images from Bill Morrison's *Decasia*, courtesy of Hypnotic Pictures.

page 15: Photo by Clifton A. Bazar, whose website is at www.pbase.com/klyphton.

page 16: "Time Has Come Today" was written by Joseph and Willie Chambers, and originally recorded by The Chambers Brothers on their 1967 album *The Time Has Come* (Columbia Records). Steve Earle's version of the song is recorded on his album *Sidetracks*, released in 2002 by Artemis Records.

page 17: This quotation is taken from a speech Abbie Hoffman delivered at Washington Place in April of 1970, at a rally on behalf of imprisoned Black Panthers.

page 18: An earlier version of this poem appeared in Forché's 2003 poetry collection *Blue Hour*, published by HarperCollins.

page 19: This essay is based on the 2004 T. S. Eliot lecture given by Don Paterson and originally commissioned by the South Bank Centre in London, England.

page 34–36: Three photographs from the show "Isaacs Seen," (a retrospective on Av Isaacs: Half a Century on the Art Front) exhibited until the end of the summer at the Justina M. Barnicke Gallery (Hart House), University of Toronto Art Centre, Textile Museum of Canada, and Art Gallery of Ontario.

page 45: Photo by Sue Schenk.

page 49: Courtesy of Oliver Sitwell.

page 49: This essay was originally published in the January 5, 2005, issue of *SF Weekly*, and also appeared in the *Anderson Valley Advertiser*.

page 50: We at *Brick*, being slightly behind in our advanced mathematics, asked Roger Bland to explain what the formula reproduced on this page actually means. This is what he told us:

"Most of us who teach or do research in Physics have to develop a way of presenting equations and formulas in publications, teaching materials, and presentations. There are several different software paths to take, and people argue constantly over which one is best. You might know LaTeX [sure we do—ed.]—it is supposed to have evolved from software used in the printing trade for electronic typesetting, and is generally preferred by purists.

"Last Christmas we had a competition to see who could take a long, complicated equation and turn it into a JPEG in the shortest time. The entrants included four Physics and Astronomy professors, and several students. They were given a handwritten version of the equation and worked against time. The contest was won by a student, using Mathematica, in the time of six minutes. (My time was about twelve minutes.)

"Here is what the equation represents as I sent it to you. On the left-hand side of the equation is a capital *psi*, a symbol representing the quantum-mechanical wave function for a single-electron atom. The subscripts (*n*, *l*, and *m*) are the quantum numbers for the state of the electron. On the other side is the actual wave function, in terms of standard mathematical functions like exponentials and factorials. It is almost scientifically correct; the one thing that was added to make it seem more complicated is the summation sign (the capital *sigma*) in the middle of the equation. The real object was to have a challenging equation to type in and format that was "typical," and no one at the time objected to the summation sign!

"I am not sure exactly who constitutes your readership. But I suspect you would not have many nasty letters to the editor if you captioned it something like this:

"'Equation used in the contest, supposed to represent the quantum-mechanical wave function for an energy eigenstate of the hydrogen atom.'

"Any reader who writes in, 'So why is that summation sign there?' will no doubt feel very good about herself!"

page 52: Originally delivered as a lecture at the Maier Museum of Art symposium *Reinterpreting Landscape* in 1996, this essay first appeared in print in Rackstraw Downes's collection *In Relation to the Whole: Three Essays from Three Decades, 1973, 1981, 1996* (pub-

lished in 2000 by Edgewise Press). Reprinted by permission of the author.

page 56–57: *U.S. Scrap Metal Gets Shipped For Reprocessing in S.E. Asia, Jersey City, N.J.* Copyright © Rackstraw Downes. Courtesy of the Betty Cuningham Gallery, New York.

page 60: This essay originally appeared in the February 13, 2005, edition of *The Telegraph* in Calcutta, India. Reprinted by permission of the author.

page 63: Selections from this piece have appeared in the articles "Living Through a War in Baghdad," published in the *Globe and Mail* on March 20, 2003, and in "Iraqi Relatives Live in Darkness and Thirst," published in the *Georgia Straight* between July 24–31, 2003.

page 66, 69: Photos by Farah Nosh.

page 76–80: Photos by kind permission of The Royal Society of Medicine.

page 95, 117, 170: Drawings by Abbey Huggan.

page 97: These diary entries are excerpted from Donald Richie's *Japan Journals*, published by Stone Bridge Press in 2004. Used by permission of the author.

page 98: Donald Richie with Susan Sontag, 1995. Courtesy of Donald Richie.

page 101: Donald Richie with Jim Jarmusch, 1990. Courtesy of Donald Richie.

page 102: Drawing by Martin Berkovitz; poem courtesy of Mary Hooper, literary executor for Milton Acorn. This artwork was originally commissioned for the Spring 1963 issue of *The Fiddlehead*.

page 104: This interview originally aired on March 17 and 24, 2005, on the KCRW radio program *Bookworm*.

page 107: Photo by George Duncan. Courtesy of St. Martin's Press/Picador.

page 129–130: Courtesy of Michael Elcock.

page 131: Photo by Rick/Simon.

page 139, 142: Photos courtesy of Vasco Ray.

page 148–149: Photo by David Donald.

page 153: Quotations are taken from Ernest Heming-way's short story "Big Two-Hearted River, Part I," first anthologized in his 1925 collection *In Our Time*. Copyright © 1925 Charles Scribner's Sons. Renewal copyright © 1955 Ernest Hemingway.

page 159: Public domain image from *The Age of Coal* CD-ROM, courtesy of *Wegway*.

page 162: Courtesy of the *Sunday Star* (Auckland, New Zealand, 1995) and New Directions.

page 165: By Robert Creeley, from *Mirrors*, copyright ©1983 by Robert Creeley. Reprinted by permission of New Directions Publishing Corp.

Special thanks to Janet Inksetter; Sally, Roger, and Emma Bland; Sushi; Annie Nocenti; Soraya Hassim; stef lenk; Isabel Huggan.

POETRY

GRIFFIN
POETRY PRIZE
2005 SHORTLIST

Photo by Shin Sugino

CANADIAN
$50,000 PRIZE

Roo Borson
*Short Journey Upriver
Toward Ōishida*
MCCLELLAND &
STEWART LTD.

George Bowering
Changing on the Fly
POLESTAR/
RAINCOAST BOOKS

Don McKay
Camber
MCCLELLAND &
STEWART LTD.

**GRIFFIN POETRY PRIZE
AWARDS EVENING**
JUNE 2, 2005

SHORTLIST READINGS
JUNE 1, 2005, 7:30PM
MacMillan Theatre, Toronto
Tickets available at
www.griffinpoetryprize.com/tickets or call 905-565-5993

INTERNATIONAL
$50,000 PRIZE

Fanny Howe
On the Ground
GRAYWOLF PRESS

**Michael Symmons
Roberts**
Corpus
JONATHAN CAPE

Matthew Rohrer
A Green Light
VERSE PRESS

Charles Simic
Selected Poems 1963-2003
FABER & FABER

Judges
Simon Armitage, Erín Moure
Tomaz Salamun

THE GRIFFIN TRUST
For Excellence In Poetry

FOR MORE INFORMATION, VISIT
WWW.GRIFFINPOETRYPRIZE.COM

Creative: Scott Thornley + Company Inc. www.st-c.com

International Readings at Harbourfront Centre

The place to hear and meet writers year-round.

Join us in June as we present Umberto Eco, Michael Cunningham, Amitav Ghosh, Anne Hines and Mark Kurlansky.

ALOUD:
a Celebration for Young Readers
June 24-26, 2005

Three days of free literary programming for the entire family. Participants include Frank Beddor, Mem Fox, Sheree Fitch, Mary Hoffman, Susan Juby, Clem Martini, Ridley Pearson, Brian MacFarlane, Jacqueline Wilson with more to be confirmed.

26th annual International Festival of Authors
October 19-29, 2005

Some of the world's most respected authors and promising literary voices gather for readings, interviews, talks, round table discussions and award presentations.

Visit **www.readings.org** for additional information and complete lineup.

INTERNATIONAL READINGS
⊙ **Harbourfront centre**

THE GLOBE AND MAIL

THE HUMBER SCHOOL FOR WRITERS

The Humbe
School for Wri
Summer Work

July 16 – July 22, 200

This summer's outstanding facul

David Bezmozgis   **Paul Qua**
Wayson Choy   **Nino Ric**
Erika de Vasconcelos   **Richard**
Bruce Jay Friedman   **Olive Se**
Isabel Huggan   **D. M. Th**
Alistair MacLeod   **Barry Ur**
John Metcalf   **Guy Van**
Kim Moritsugu   **Richard**

Special Guest: **Ha**

Antanas Sileika   416-675-6622 ex
antanas.sileika@humber.ca

 **HUMBER**
School of Creative & Performing Arts   http://creativear
Toronto, Ontario

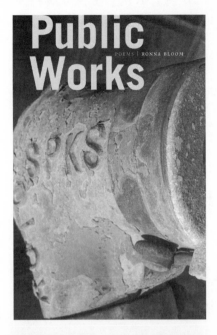

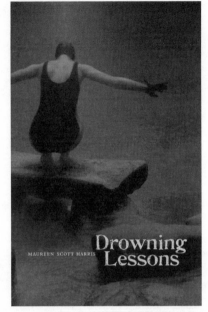

PUBLIC WORKS
poems by RONNA BLOOM
ISBN 0-9732140-2-3
112 pages $19.95 paper

DROWNING LESSONS
poems by MAUREEN SCOTT HARRIS
ISBN 0-9732140-8-2
104 pages $21.00 paper

SMALL ARGUMENTS
poems by SOUVANKHAM THAMMAVONGSA
ISBN 0-9732140-5-8
64 pages $17.95 paper

STORMY WEATHER: FOURSOMES
poems by STAN DRAGLAND
ISBN 1-897141-01-7
64 pages $25.00 cloth

Now Represented by
THE LITERARY PRESS GROUP
416.483.1321
www.lpg.ca

PEDLAR
PRESS

BETH FOLLETT *Publisher* P.O. BOX 26, Station P Toronto, Ontario Canada M5S 2S6 (416) 534-2011

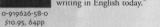

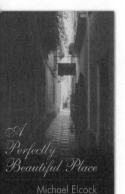

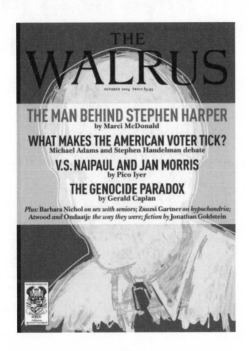

An Immodest Proposal

WHAT IS THERE in this crazy mixed-up world that you can count on any more if it isn't love? Birds and bees do it, the monkeys in the trees do it, so let's do it too, let's—

Well, hold on a second. You're a person and we're a magazine. The kids might look funny. But you have to admit, you feel it too, don't you? Every sixth month or so, you wonder how we're doing, if we're thinking of you, when you might see us again. It's gotta be love. Can you live without us? Then say no more. Let's make a commitment. Just the two of us. And, er, anyone else who might be into it. *Brick* is now offering ten-year Sponsor Subscriptions. When's the last time someone offered you ten years? It's almost like marriage, only not as scary, and hell, if we like the first decade together, we can do it again.

What do you get out of this? You get the magazine uninterrupted for an entire decade; you get your name in the magazine in our Sponsor Subscribers' section for the entire period (just like all those folks whose names you see on page 174 of this very issue . . . hey thanks, 333 ANON!); but most of all, you get the knowledge that you're pledging your support to *Brick* in a concrete and sustaining way.

You can join us for ten continuous years of *Brick* for CDN$195 in Canada (that's a 25 per cent savings off the newsstand price), US$215 in the United States (a 15 per cent savings off the newsstand price), or US$240 overseas (an incalculable savings, since you'll be hard pressed to find us on most foreign newsstands!). Buying a ten-year subscription protects you against all subscription- or postal-rate increases over the entire period (with the proviso that if you move from Calgary to Latvia the month after subscribing, we might have to contact you about postal costs). And think how smart you'll feel in 2012 when Brick costs $90 an issue. You'll practically be *making* money.

But wait, there's more. And we're not talking *Crying Game* here. We're just thinking you might want to exchange tokens of affection. When you fill out the back of this card, you'll see some gift options, each of which comes with a corresponding gift from us. It's not obligatory (your love will always be enough), but we know you want to keep us in the manner to which we've been long praying to become accustomed.

Whatever it is that you love about us—and we've already said the feeling is mutual, haven't we?—we hope you'll help us keep the sparks flying.

❏ Yes, I want to join BRICK on this ten-year adventure of love. I'm enclosing at least:

❏ CDN$195, for a Canadian subscription (including GST)—25% off the newsstand price

❏ US$215, for a U.S. subscription—15% off the newsstand price

❏ US$240, for an overseas subscription—an incalculable savings (we're not on foreign newsstands!)

Name (if a gift, fill out recipient's address) _____

Address _____

_____

E-mail _____ Telephone _____

❏ This is a NEW subscription   ❏ This extends a CURRENT subscription

❏ This is a GIFT from _____

❏ Please list my name on the Sponsor Subscribers' section as follows:
_____ (If left blank, purchaser's name will be used. If you wish
to be anonymous, please write "Anonymous" here.)

In addition to my subscription, I would like to make BRICK a gift of:

❏ $50, in the hope that BRICK will be able to afford more semi-colons. I will be pleased to accept a literary gift from the magazine in exchange.

❏ $100, in order to effect the immediate purchase of a larger supply of #2 HB pencils (preferred brand: Hello Kitty). I will be delighted to receive the above gift, plus a second, personalized literary gift from the magazine.

❏ $250, because I am concerned Jim Harrison is limiting his intake of Didier Dagueneau's Pouilly-Fumé Silex. In addition to the above gifts, I will receive two complimentary tickets to all public BRICK events for the whole period of my subscription.

❏ BRICK, I love you and I'm thrilled we're finally getting married. Go to Vera Wang's and buy yourself the most lavish wedding gown you can get for $____ (minimum CDN$500). You'll get dolled up, and I'll get all of the above, plus an invitation to a special Sponsors' Dinner to be held early in 2006.

❏ No, I don't want a ten-year subscription, but I'm still filling out this card and wasting a stamp because I suffer from strange compulsions.

Now . . . tear out this card and send it to: BRICK, Box 537, Stn Q, Toronto, Ontario M4T 2M5, Canada
Or visit us on the Web at WWW.BRICKMAG.COM, and click on our Sponsor Subscription link!

THE FINE PRINT. This offer ends December 31, 2005. BRICK is not a registered charity—even though BRICK staff might feel as if it were!—and unfortunately cannot issue tax receipts.

TYS200505

Lay down your weary head.
We'll bring *Brick* right to your bedside (almost) for two years . . .

Please send me two years (four issues) of BRICK. I'm including:
❏ $38 for Canada ❏ US$41 for the United States ❏ US$46 elsewhere
(including GST)

Name

Address

E-mail   Telephone

❏ This is a NEW subscription ❏ This is a RENEWAL

Nobody who cares about books or life could be disappointed in Brick. — Alice Munro

Open some new doors for a loved one. Give them *Brick*.

Please send someone I like two years (four issues) of BRICK. I'm including:
❏ $38 for Canada ❏ US$41 for the United States ❏ US$46 elsewhere
(including GST)

Name

Address

E-mail   Telephone

Your name

❏ Begin gift with current issue ❏ Begin gift with next issue

Brick is one of the best journals of ideas published in the English-speaking world. — Russell Banks

PLEASE INCLUDE THIS CARD WITH YOUR
PAYMENT AND MAIL TO:

BRICK
BOX 537, STN Q
TORONTO, ONTARIO   M4T 2M5
CANADA

PLEASE INCLUDE THIS CARD WITH YOUR
PAYMENT AND MAIL TO:

BRICK
BOX 537, STN Q
TORONTO, ONTARIO   M4T 2M5
CANADA